Athens Streets & Neighborhoods

Athens Streets & Neighborhoods

The Origins of Some Street Names and
Place Names in Athens, Georgia

Gary L. Doster

Deeds Publishing | Athens

Copyright © 2021 — Gary L. Doster

ALL RIGHTS RESERVED—No part of this book may be reproduced in any form or by any electronic or mechanical means, including information storage and retrieval systems, without permission in writing from the authors, except by a reviewer who may quote brief passages in a review.

Published by Deeds Publishing in Athens, GA
www.deedspublishing.com

Printed in The United States of America

Cover design by Mark Babcock.

ISBN 978-1-950794-30-0

Books are available in quantity for promotional or premium use. For information, email info@deedspublishing.com or www.athenshistorical.org.

First Edition, 2021

10 9 8 7 6 5 4 3 2 1

Thanks to my dear wife, Faye, who continues to tolerate my obsession with history after being together for more than 61 years.

This book was funded by the Athens Historical Society.

Books are available at www.athenshistorical.org.

Contents

Acknowledgments — ix

Foreword — xi

Introduction — xv

Some Athens Streets — 1

Some Athens Communities and Neighborhoods — 83

References — 107

Illustrations — 111

Index — 135

About the Author — 163

Acknowledgments

Most of all, I thank Dr. Dottie Kimbrell Mercer, who conducted a thorough, meticulous search of an early draft of this manuscript and routed out many mistakes in grammar, punctuation, verb tense, and sentence structure and found a few misidentified names and some misspelled words. She also tutored me along the way on several occasions to help make this book as good as possible. Dottie is a true master of the English language and a good friend.

Another good friend who helped more than she knows is Eve Mayes. In addition to being an excellent researcher, writer, and editor, Eve probably knows more about the mechanics of using a computer than anyone else I know. Eve came to my aid and rescued me on several occasions when I encountered problems I did not understand and could not fix on my own.

Thanks to Dr. Dave Anderson for his review of the manuscript and his helpful and constructive criticism for its improvement.

Appreciation is extended to Sam Thomas, curator of the T.R.R. Cobb House and president of the Athens Historical Society, who provided considerable editorial assistance, but most important, he was mainly responsible for the Athens Historical Society publishing this book.

Others who helped include Dan Aldrich, Wayne Arnold, Patsy Hawkins Arnold, Ron Bogue, Nancy Bunker Bowen, Steven Brown, Rikki Chesley, Peggy Galis, Theresa Graham, Frank Jackson, Mary Linnemann, Charlotte Thomas Marshall, Edwin H. Oldham, Kristen Smith, Angela Stanley, Mary Claire Warren, Lisabeth Wells-Pratt, Homer Wilson, and Donna E. Wood. Some of these folks helped a little bit and some of them helped a lot; I am grateful to them all.

And I am certainly grateful to Bob, Jan, Mark, and Matt, the folks at Deed's Publishing for their outstanding assistance on many occasions. They went far beyond what is usually expected from someone serving as publisher, and they made the book better in many ways. They are a pleasure to work with.

And special thanks to Coach Vince Dooley for the wonderful Foreword he provided. I really appreciate him doing this. To me, it is the highlight of the book!

Foreword

Gary Doster, respected and beloved historian, continues his lifelong pursuit of Athens and Georgia history by producing another informative book of the Classic City. With typical diligent Doster research, he has provided for the Clarke County community in this book *Athens Streets & Neighborhoods*, a ready reference to *The Origin of Some Street Names and Place Names in Athens, Georgia*.

I was flattered, though with some reluctance, when Mr. Doster asked me through our mutual friend Sam Thomas to write the foreword to this book. My initial hesitancy quickly turned to excitement upon learning the first primary source in Doster's research came from a committee appointed by the Athens City Council in 1859. A key member of the street-naming committee was William Gaston Delony (1826-1863). Sam Thomas and I teamed up for several years getting to know this Confederate Calvary Colonel "Fighting Bulldog," the main protagonist of a book we wrote together.

Writing this foreword has given me a deeper appreciation for the exceptional work Doster has done in the past in researching and writing about the city of Athens and the state of Georgia.

Members of the Athens Historical Society have long recognized his work and in 2019 honored him as the winner of the Hull Award for his "significant contribution to the knowledge of Athens' history."

In addition to the original 1859 committee report, Doster scrutinized numerous publications for tidbits about the subject. To his surprise, he found some three thousand streets by various names but wisely decided to deal "with only a small percentage of them," two hundred and forty to be exact. In the book, he also discusses thirty neighborhoods or communities in Clarke County. Supplementing this entire study, Doster made good use of Athens maps drawn in 1874 and 1895.

As might be understandable, most all of the streets in the city were named in honor of white men. One of the few exceptions is STANTON WAY, named in honor of Lucy May Stanton (1875-1931) who became a world famous artist. She spent the last twenty years of her life in Athens advocating for women's rights. She died in 1931 and is buried in Oconee Hill Cemetery.

There are streets named after many more notables such as BALDWIN STREET, after Abraham Baldwin, the University of Georgia's first president. There is also BARROW STREET, named for David C. Barrow, Jr. (1852-1929), who was Chancellor of the University of Georgia from 1906 to 1925. He was so well loved and respected that a county in Georgia is also named after him. One of Athens' longest streets, MILLEDGE AVENUE (almost five miles long), running from Prince Avenue to Whitehall is named for John Milledge (1757-1815) who bought and donated the land for the establishment of the University of Georgia and Athens. He became governor of the state and a United States Senator, and Milledgeville, one-time capital of the state, is also named in his honor. I would be remiss not to mention HERTY DRIVE, named in honor of Dr. Charles H. Herty, a renowned chemistry professor and "father of football" at the University of Georgia.

Besides the streets named for many Athens notables, a few others that Doster mentions are worth highlighting. BROAD STREET is one of the most well-known streets in Athens as well as many other cities throughout the country. It was once called FRONT STREET "because it ran in *front* of the University." BOBBIN MILL ROAD was named after an industry that was known throughout the south and northeast in the late nineteenth and early twentieth century. The water-powered mill stood on Brooklyn Branch and manufactured bobbins (from dogwood trees) for textile mills all over the south and eastern United States.

Lastly, I must mention PLUM NELLY ROAD. Doster heard the story as a youngster, as I did when I first came to Athens in 1963. Located just north of West Lake Drive, it forms a circle before terminating at Rocky Ford Road. The street was so named because it was "Plum out of town, and nelly out of the county." Doster, who can't verify the story, but has "always believed it," has convinced me not to challenge the tale.

Finally, Doster breaks down several communities and neighborhoods in the county. I am somewhat familiar with some of the thirty that he listed such as the prestigious COBBHAM, (Cobb Ham) which borders Prince Avenue. I have long heard of other historic neighborhoods such as NORMAL TOWN, HOT CORNER, PRINCETON, and CARR'S HILL. I am familiar with the fact that in 1913 MILLEDGE CIRCLE was developed to join the intersection of Milledge Avenue and Lumpkin Street to create the now very popular FIVE POINTS.

What I was not familiar with, but has now stirred my curiosity, is the BROOKLYN COMMUNITY and THE BROOKLYN

Gary L. Doster

CEMETARY less than one-half mile from our home on Milledge Circle. Learning about the Brooklyn Community and Cemetery and other revealing facts of the city was a special benefit to me of reading Doster's book. It has enhanced my knowledge and continuing love for a community that Barbara and I have had the good fortune of living in and raising a family for some fifty-five of our sixty years of marriage.

One can tell that this book was a labor of love on a topic that has long held an interest to the author. Doster's painstaking and thorough research show on each page of this work, and it belongs on the shelf of anyone interested in the history of Athens and Clarke County. Thank you, Gary, for another significant contribution to Athens' most interesting and intriguing history.

—Vince Dooley

Introduction

Newcomers to Athens often wonder (and often ask) how certain streets and neighborhoods got their names. Most lifelong residents of Athens do not know the origins of these names either. Some appear obvious, but others, after much searching, remain a mystery. In present-day Athens-Clarke County, there are almost 3,000 avenues, boulevards, circles, courts, crossings, drives, extensions, lanes, passes, places, points, roads, runs, streets, terraces, traces, trails, walks, and ways, but I am going to deal with only a small percentage of them. It has been difficult to decide which streets to include and which to leave out. I decided to stay mainly with the old original part of downtown Athens where many of the streets were named for early prominent citizens, but I made a few exceptions. I included some newer streets because we know the identity of the people for whom they were named, and I want to record them before the information is lost for future generations. I have avoided most of those streets named for "things," e.g. Branch, Oak, River, Vine, First, Second, Third, etc., but, here again, I made a few exceptions.

I considered listing only those streets that still exist, but there is too much Athens history associated with some of those old, obsolete streets to leave them out. A number of streets that appear on some early maps of Athens never existed except "on paper." Some are included even though they were not developed. In addition to street names, I have also included a number of Athens place names because some are historically significant.

The source of many of the street names is understood; others are informed guesses. One would assume that the most prominent Athenian with the "right" name was the person for whom the street was named. I have not attempted to provide a detailed biography on each person for whom a street was named but merely endeavored to identify them. For more information on the people, see the list of suggested references at the end of this book.

The Athens City Council officially named many of the town's existing streets at their meeting on April 2, 1859. The *Southern Banner* published their report, "Streets of Athens, as named by the Council of 1859" on April 7 (p. 2). The 1859 list included 46 streets, of which many had been named many years previously; other names apparently were selected by the committee and appeared for the first time. Each street that had been named was listed, along with where it began and ended, and some descriptions even included the names of some well-known residents or businesses on the street. This list gave no information on the identity of the person for whom the street was named; however, some are quite obvious. There are some discrepancies between the actual minutes and the account published in the *Southern Banner*, so I used the version in the minutes.

The members of the committee were Chairman, Alonzo Alexander Franklin Hill (1826-1872), Asaph King Childs (1820-1902), and William Gaston Delony (1826-1863). They reported that "The Committee to whom was referred the naming of the streets of Athens have discharged that duty, and have the honor to submit for your approval the subjoined report. It will be seen that streets with well-known names have had them retained. The design in the others has been to perpetuate the names of some of the early citizens of our town—particularly of those now dead—and also of some who have done service to the University of Georgia and the State." The list of 46 streets followed in random order.

Several earlier authors published articles on Athens street names. In 1919, UGA professor Dr. Sylvanus Morris published an article in the December 26 issue of the *Weekly Banner* entitled "History of the Names of the Streets of Athens." Dr. Morris listed 34 early Athens streets and gave the names of the men for whom he thought they were named. Morris listed 28 of the streets that were on the 1859 committee's list, but six were not (Bloomfield, Church, Harris, Reese, States Rights/Henderson, and White).

The next reference I found regarding the names of Athens streets was published in 1923 in *History of Athens & Clarke County, Georgia*, by Hugh Jackson Rowe (1869-1945), former mayor of Athens (1910-11 and 1912-13). Rowe listed the names of 36 Athens streets, and for most of them he identified the individual for whom he thought each was named. Rowe's list contains eight streets that were not on the 1859 committee's list because they either did not exist at that time or had not been named. (Bloomfield, Childs, Church, Grady, Harris, Reese, States Rights/Henderson, Reese, and White). Rowe's list included all but two of the streets that Morris had listed in his 1919 newspaper article (Mitchell and Newton), plus three that Morris did not list (Broad, Childs, and Grady). Most would agree with the majority of Morris' and Rowe's conclusions when they identified the person for whom a street was named, but there are a few that are questionable.

Gary L. Doster

In September 1948, Thomas Walter Reed (1870-1950), UGA registrar and secretary-treasurer of the UGA Board of Trustees, published a two-part article in the *Banner-Herald* entitled "Echoes from Memoryland, How a Number of the Older Streets in Athens Got Their Names." Reed discussed most of the same streets that had been treated previously by Morris in 1919 and Rowe in 1923. However, the greatest difference in Reed's articles and those published by Morris and Rowe was that he included considerably more detail on most of the individuals for whom a street was named.

Athenian Jones Milner Drewry (1922-2014) authored an article in the December 12, 1963, issue of the *Athens Banner-Herald* entitled "Our Street Names, A Key to Athens' History is Given." Drewry listed 38 old Athens streets and gave the names of the individuals for whom he thought they were named. Drewry's list contained most of the same names that previous writers had recorded, and he listed the same individuals they did as being the persons for whom the various streets were named.

In March 1978, Dr. John Algeo, UGA Professor Emeritus of English, published a paper entitled "From Classic to Classy—Changing Fashions in Street Names" (*Names: A Journal of Onomastics*, Vol. 26, Issue 1, pp. 88-95), in which he listed and discussed the 46 streets that the 1859 committee had listed, along with a few that came into existence later. Then Dr. Algeo discussed some newer, modern streets in four contiguous subdivisions and an apartment complex in Athens and elaborated on how they were named. Thirty-seven years later, in 2015, Dr. Algeo reprinted this same article in the same publication (*Names: A Journal of Onomastics*, Vol. 63, Issue 4, pp. 220-232).

There is a brief treatment of Athens street names in *Athens Georgia Celebrating 200 Years at the Millennium*, published in 1999.

Athens Streets & Neighborhoods

This beautiful and informative tome was written by Conoly Hester with contributions by her husband, Al Hester, and includes photographs by Terry Allen. Conoly devoted only one page to the subject of street names and listed only ten old streets but she raised an important question: Why was there never a street named for Daniel Easley, one of the earliest settlers of this area who sold the land to John Milledge where Athens and the University of Georgia were sited?

In addition to the published lists from 1859 to 2015, the 1874 map of Athens drawn by William Winstead Thomas (1849-1904) and the 1895 map of Athens drawn by John William Barnett (1868-1962) were studied. The 1874 Thomas map was reprinted by the Athens Historical Society in 1974, and the 1895 Barnett map was reprinted in 1982 by The Department of Geography, Institute of Community and Area Development, and Cartographic Services Laboratory of the University of Georgia. Excerpts from both maps were used as figures in this treatise. Many streets named on these maps were not included on the lists from 1859 to 2015. Furthermore, in reading the names of streets listed in some early editions of the *Athens City Directory*, a few more names were discovered and added to the list.

Invaluable to this project was the Athens Historic Newspapers Archive posted online by The Digital Library of Georgia (http://athnewspapers.galileo.usg.edu/athnewspapers-j2k/search). This allowed me to easily search the Athens newspapers from the January 26, 1827, issue of the *Athenian* to the December 31, 1928, issue of the *Athens Banner-Herald*. Although many issues are missing and some are nearly illegible, nevertheless, these old daily and weekly newspapers provided a unique source of information not available anywhere else. Throughout the text, I have inserted comments regarding the first time I have found a newspaper reference to a place name or a street. This is not intended to imply that this is when the street or place was created; it simply is to provide a reference that otherwise may not be available.

I combined all the lists from 1859 to the present, and they are presented here alphabetically, along with the names of additional streets and neighborhoods gleaned from Thomas' 1874 map, Barnett's 1895 map, and early issues of the *Athens City Directory*. The list presented below totals more than 240 Athens streets and more than 30 neighborhood or community names. I have listed the streets and neighborhoods separately.

As would be expected, almost all of these street names and community names were selected to honor white adult males. But there are a few exceptions, including the first names and maiden names of some ladies and even a five-year-old girl!

There is no doubt about the accuracy of the origins of most of these names, but for some we may never know for sure. However, I included many of the "unknowns" in the hope that it might inspire some future researcher to pursue this project further.

Athens Streets & Neighborhoods

Some Athens Streets

Adams Street and **Habersham Street** are identified on W. W. Thomas' 1874 map of Athens as the only named streets in a new subdivision on Milledge Avenue between present-day Rutherford Street and Five Points (See Fig. 2). The subdivision was called "Adams Estate." This subdivision and these streets may have existed only on Thomas' map and not in reality. Adams Street most likely was named for Flournoy Woodbridge "Ferdy" Adams (c.1840-1874), a one-term mayor of Athens in 1861. Adams married Emma E. Barnett in 1857. During the War Between the States, Adams was Captain of the Lipscomb Volunteers, a local home defense unit comprised primarily of older citizens, including most of the UGA faculty. After the war, when the National Bank of Athens was founded in 1866, Adams was Cashier. Adams moved to New York in about 1872 and died of smallpox there on November 14, 1874. Habersham Street probably was named for Ferdy's brother, Habersham J. Adams (1827-1898), a Methodist preacher. It is possible that Adams Street also was named for Habersham and not his brother, Ferdy. Habersham Adams served the Georgia Methodist Conference for 43 years before retiring and moving to St. Louis, Missouri, to live with some of his children. He died there shortly thereafter, and his remains were returned to Athens and buried in Oconee Hill Cemetery. Adams Street and Habersham Street no longer exist by those names, but Adams Street appears to be present-day Woodlawn Avenue, and Habersham Street appears to be present-day Oakland Avenue. The first reference I found for Woodlawn Avenue was in the *Weekly Banner*, February 7, 1913, and the first reference found for Oakland Avenue was in the *Athens Banner*, March 12, 1913.

Ambler Road is located in Oconee Heights and apparently traverses part of the former route of Auslund Avenue and Rhodes Street. See Oconee Heights in the section on Athens Communities and Neighborhoods for more information.

Armory Road was originally named Water Street, but the name was changed in 1862 when Ferdinand and Francis Cook moved their machinery to Athens from New Orleans and built Cook and Brother Armory to manufacture guns for the Confederacy during the War Between the States. After the war, the name was changed back to Water Street. The route now is named Dr. Martin Luther King, Jr. Parkway. See Water Street for information on another Athens street with this name.

Augusta Alley formerly was named Bernside Alley. It is assumed that the name Augusta came from the Georgia town of that name, but the origin of the name Bernside was not determined. This alleyway ran east from Augusta Avenue to Macon Avenue in Newtown (or New Town) community. (See Fig. 10). Augusta Alley no longer exists.

Athens Streets & Neighborhoods

Auslund Avenue is located in Oconee Heights and named for C. Fred Auslund. Auslund Avenue formed the western boundary of Auslund's estate, Oconee Heights. Part of the street apparently still exists as Ambler Road. See Oconee Heights in the section on Athens Communities and Neighborhoods for more information.

Bacon Street no longer exists. It was a two-block-long street that ran east and west from College Avenue to the North Oconee River. The street may have been named for Dr. William Bacon, a well-known and successful Athens druggist and dentist in the mid-19th century. However, it most likely was named for Augustus Octavius Bacon (1839-1914), who graduated from the University of Georgia in 1859 and received his law degree from UGA in 1860. He became a U.S. senator in 1894 and served until his death in 1914. Bacon County, Georgia, was named for him. The first reference found for Bacon Street was in the *Weekly Banner* April 5, 1912.

Bailey Street (also seen as Bailey Row) probably was named in honor of Thomas Bailey (1839-1922), but that has not been confirmed. Bailey moved here from Tennessee as a young man and worked at the Athens Steam Company, later renamed Athens Foundry and Machine Works. Bailey was working at the foundry in 1863 when Athens' famous double-barreled cannon was cast there. Bailey later became foreman of the foundry. Bailey Street is an old street in East Athens that begins on Oconee Street and runs southwest. It was shortened considerably when the Athens bypass was built in recent times. The first reference found for Bailey Street was in the *Weekly Banner*, Oct. 12, 1900. There also currently is a Bailey Street that runs northeast off Prince Avenue just inside the Athens bypass in the northwestern part of town. This one-block-long, dead-end street is not known to have any connection to the Bailey Street in East Athens.

Baker Street is located in East Athens and runs northeast from Vine Street to Fairview Street. The origin of this street name was not determined but in some early issues of the Athens City Directory, there was a carriage maker named Ernest Baker and a tinner named Grover Baker who lived nearby on Peter Street; perhaps it was named for one or both of them or some former member of their family. The first reference found for Baker Street was in the *Athens Banner-Herald* August 3, 1923.

Baldwin Street was named for Abraham Baldwin (1754-1807), who proposed the bill in the Georgia Legislature under which the University of Georgia was authorized and chartered. (See Fig. 8 and 15) Baldwin was the first president of the university (1785-1801), but during his sixteen-year tenure the university existed only on paper. Although some people often write that "Franklin College became the University of Georgia," or that "the name of Franklin College was changed to the University of Georgia," neither of these claims is true; it has always been The University of Georgia. A university is comprised of colleges, just as colleges are made up of schools, and schools are a compilation of departments. Franklin College just happened to be the first (and for a while the only) college in the university. Baldwin, Georgia, Baldwin County, Georgia, and Baldwin Hall on the UGA campus also were named for Abraham Baldwin. He served in various political offices during his lifetime, including Georgia state representative, U.S. representative, and U.S. senator. The first reference found for Baldwin Street was in the *Southern Whig*, April 29, 1847.

Barber Street, according to Rowe (1923), was named for Greensby Wetherford "Wed" Barber (1818-1883), born at Barber Springs (later named Linton Springs, now covered by the Athens bypass). Barber's name also has been seen spelled Weathersby. He died in Barberville Community (also named for him) on North Avenue.

Barnett Shoals Road no doubt was named for Revolutionary War soldier John Barnett (1762-1814), an early settler in the area. Barnett built a fort overlooking the Oconee River near the site where the Star Thread Factory later was built (1890). The thread factory was just upstream from where Barnett Shoals Dam was built by the Georgia Power Company in 1909-1910. Barnett is buried in a small family cemetery on a bluff above the river near the site of his former home. He has a tombstone that was provided by the U.S. Veterans Administration and placed there many years ago by the Daughters of the American Revolution. Also see Bob Godfrey Road.

Barrett Street later was changed to Ruth Street. This street begins after crossing the North Oconee River on present-day Elizabeth Street. Ruth Street continues northward to connect with River Street/Water Street/Madison Avenue/North Avenue. It is thought that Barrett Street was named for Barrett Phinizy, one of the sons of Ferdinand Phinizy. See Phinizy Street for additional information on Ferdinand Phinizy.

Barrow Street was named for David Crenshaw Barrow, Jr. (1852-1929), Chancellor of the University of Georgia from 1906 to 1925. Barrow was one of the most loved and respected men of his time. Barrow Elementary School in Athens and Barrow County, Georgia, also were named for him, as was Barrow Hall on the UGA campus.

Baxter Drive probably was named for Thomas W. Baxter. See Baxter Street for further information.

Baxter Street was named for Thomas W. Baxter (1787-1844), who came to Athens from Hancock County, Georgia, in 1831. He was a successful merchant and later was in charge of the Athens Manufacturing Company. Baxter served in the Seminole Indian War, and six of his sons served in the Confederate Army during the War Between the States.

Becker Street was the former name of present-day Florida Avenue. The origin of the name of Becker Street was not determined, but John H. Becker and his wife, Carrie, were listed in the 1912-13 *Athens City Directory* as living on this street; perhaps it was named for him. The first reference found for Becker Street was in the *Athens Banner*, January 6, 1910.

Bernside Alley was changed to Augusta Alley. The origin of the name of either was not determined. The alley was located in Newtown (or New Town) and connected Augusta Avenue with Macon Avenue. It no longer exists.

Berry Street originally was named Hodgson Street but was changed to Berry Street on February 6, 1908. It was a one-block-long street on the west side of the North Oconee River leading to the bridge, connecting Strong Street to Bridge Street. The street no longer exists. Also see Hodgson Street.

Billups Street was named for Col. John Billups (1802-1872), a prominent citizen of Athens. Billups attended UGA and then studied law at Princeton College and Union College. When he returned to Georgia, he was elected to public office and served as Speaker of the Georgia House of Representatives and President of the Georgia Senate. Billups was commissioned as aide-de-camp to John Forsyth (1780-1841) during Forsyth's tenure as governor of Georgia (1827-1829), where he earned the title of Colonel. During the Seminole Indian War in South Florida, Billups served under Major General Burwell Pope. During the War Between the States, Billups was among a group of older Athenians who formed the Mitchell Thunderbolts, a home guard unit. Among his many other accomplishments, he also was a trustee of the University of Georgia. The first reference found for Billups Street was in the *Southern Banner*, July 14, 1859.

Bird Street is located in Newtown (or New Town) and runs north from Atlanta Avenue. (See Fig. 10). The origin of this street name was not determined, and it is not known if this street was named for a person or a bird. The first reference found for Bird Street was in *The Athens Banner* November 5, 1891.

Bloomfield Street was named for Robert Lee Bloomfield (1827-1916), an early Athens resident who came here from New Jersey. Bloomfield was involved in numerous business ventures with other Athens businessmen and is considered to be among Athens' most active "movers and shakers" of his time. He also was a staunch supporter of Emmanuel Episcopal Church, and he built St. Mary's Episcopal Church on Oconee Street for the benefit of his employees at Athens Factory. The first reference found for Bloomfield Street was in the *Banner Watchman*, August 18, 1885. In the April 27, 1937, issue of the *Banner-Herald*, there was a letter to the editor entitled "Mr. T. W. Reed Opposes Changing Street Name." The letter writer was Thomas Walter Reed (1870-1950) who, among other things, was registrar of the University of Georgia and was secretary-treasurer of the UGA Board of Trustees. Reed's letter was in response to a proposition before the Mayor and City Council to change the name of Bloomfield Street. Reed drafted a most eloquent and convincing letter to the newspaper, espousing his opposition to this change. In the letter, Reed recounted many good things that Bloomfield accomplished during his life in Athens. It is quite obvious that Reed was successful; the name of this street remains the same today.

Bobbin Mill Road ran from present-day Springdale Street to a water-powered mill on Brooklyn Branch that manufactured wooden bobbins for textile mills all over the eastern United States. The bobbins were fashioned mostly from dogwood trees because of the quality and resiliency of the wood. The mill was opened in the 1850s and eventually was acquired by John Hamlin Newton (1800-1889). After Newton's death, the mill came under the management of his son-in-law Dr. Henry Hull Carlton (1834-1905), who was married to Newton's daughter Helen. This was the only bobbin mill in the South, and its products were in great demand. The mill purportedly manufactured as many as 5,000 bobbins a day. In a newspaper story in the *Athens Banner* in 1894, it was reported that Dr. Carlton had received an order for 40,000 bobbins from one of the largest cotton mills in North Carolina and was engaged in producing 3,000 bobbins a day to fill the order. Bobbin Mill Road still exists, but no longer extends all the way to the site of the mill, and few people know the origin of the name.

Bob Godfrey Road serves as the county line between Clarke and Oconee counties in the southeastern part of Clarke County. It used to be part of the Barnett Shoals Road, but the name of this two-mile section was changed early in the 20th century. The first reference found for the name of the road was in a document in the Oconee County Courthouse dated 1922. The western end of the road begins at the present Barnett Shoals Road and extends eastward. It crosses Belmont Road and continues a short distance to the Oglethorpe County line, where it becomes Wolfskin Road. The road was named for Robert Wiley Godfrey (1857-1940), who served as the postmaster of the U.S. Post Office in the small Oconee County community of Rutherford near Barnett Shoals Dam. Some local residents call this little ghost town Barnett Shoals, but its legal name is Rutherford. The post office opened May 16, 1895, and closed November 29, 1902; Godfrey served as postmaster from January 12, 1897, to May 15, 1901. After his service as postmaster at Rutherford, Godfrey was a partner with four other men in the Shoal Creek Gin Company and also ran a country store on the Wire Bridge Road about a half mile from the intersection of Belmont Road and present-day Bob Godfrey Road. Godfrey's name also has been seen spelled as Godfree and Godfrie; in fact, his name and his wife's name are spelled Godfree on their tombstone in the Corinth Baptist Cemetery on Belmont Road at the intersection with Bob Godfrey Road.

Boulevard is correctly named **The Boulevard**. It is the main east-west street through the property that was developed as Athens Park and Improvement Company in the 1890s. The street extends from Barber Street on the East end to Pound Street at the West end. (See Fig. 11).

Bowdre Street is shown on Barnett's 1895 map of Athens as a one-block-long street that connected the "original" Clover Street (present-day Hillcrest Avenue) with the original Meigs Street (present-day Glenhaven Avenue). Apparently, Bowdre Street was located where present-day Matthews Avenue is located. It is thought that Bowdre Street was one of several Athens streets named for members of the Phinizy Family. Also see Barrett, Jacob, Phinizy, Leonard, and Stewart streets. (See Fig. 6).

Bray's Alley ran south from Madison Avenue/North Avenue/River Street through the property of Isham (also seen as Isom) M. Bray (1884-1955) and Nora L. Bray (1885-1962). The Brays and their extended family operated Bray's Place & Cottage Camp, an early stopover for tourists traveling through this area. Mr. and Mrs. Bray first ran a service station in the area from about 1920 but eventually expanded to a campground and motel for tourists. In their later years, they operated a mobile home park on the property. A number of their children and other relatives assisted in the operation.

Bremond Street (also seen as Bremont Street) is a two-block-long dead-end street that runs north from Strickland Street. Bremont Street is mentioned in the *Athens Daily Herald*, August 13, 1914, and it is assumed that this is the same street. The origin of the name was not determined.

Bridge Street connected Berry Street/Hodgson Street to Madison Avenue/North Avenue/River Street at the end of the bridge crossing the North Oconee River. This street no longer exists.

Brittain Avenue is a one-block-long, dead-end street that runs northwest from Lumpkin Street between the Treanor House and Bloomfield Street. The origin of this street name was not determined for certain, but it probably was named for Henry L. Brittain

(1798-1890), who moved to Athens from Oglethorpe County in the 1850s. Henry Brittain bought the currently-named Treanor House from Williams Rutherford, Jr. in 1857 and lived there for the rest of his life. This house has been known as the Treanor House since 1935, when it was bought by Mrs. Katharine McKinley Taylor Treanor. Brittain's daughter, Susan Brittain Martin, continued to own the Treanor House until 1905. The first reference found for Brittain Avenue was in the *Athens Banner*, March 7, 1912.

Broad Street was included in this list because it is among the first and most well-known streets in Athens. It first was called Front Street because it ran in the front of the University. In his *Annals of Athens, Georgia*, Hull wrote that the street also was sometimes called Public Street. The name was changed to Broad Street in 1859 when the other Athens streets received their designations by the committee on naming streets. This is one of the most popular street names in the USA, and there are literally hundreds of towns across the country with a Broad Street.

D. W. Brooks Drive begins at the intersection with East Campus Road, and is called Agriculture Drive, but as it runs north for a few blocks it becomes D. W. Brooks Drive. The street passes by the College of Engineering, the College of Veterinary Medicine, and the UGA Coliseum. At the intersection with Carlton Street there is a break in the continuity of the street for D. W. Brooks Mall, but the street resumes at the intersection with Soule Street and runs to Cedar Drive. The street and the mall were named for David William Brooks (1901-1999) from Royston, Georgia, who earned a bachelor's degree and a master's degree in agronomy from UGA. After graduation, Brooks taught agronomy at UGA before venturing out into the business world. He was very successful in business and was the founder of Gold Kist, Inc. and Cotton States Mutual Insurance Company. Brooks became famous and respected worldwide because of his expertise on policy and trade issues related to agriculture. Consequently, Brooks became an advisor to seven U.S. presidents on these topics. Brooks received many awards during his lifetime, including the Distinguished Agribusiness Award from the Georgia Agribusiness Council, and in 1966 he was named *Progressive Farmer*'s Man of the Year in Agriculture in the South. On November 4, 1972, he was the first inductee into UGA's Agricultural Hall of Fame. The D.W. Brooks Lecture Series and Faculty Awards for Excellence at UGA were established in his honor.

Brown Street was described in the 1859 committee list of street names as running "...south of Mr. Bishop's from Jackson Street to Thomas Street." It is not known for sure for whom Brown Street was named, but the most likely candidate is Dr. John Brown, third president of the University of Georgia (1811-1816). This one-block-long street ran along the northern boundary of the Old Athens Cemetery on Jackson Street (See Fig. 8). The name later was changed to Graveyard Street, then Magazine Street, then was obliterated when the UGA Visual Arts Building (now the College of Environmental Design) was constructed on Jackson Street.

Bryan Street is a one-block-long street that runs west off North Chase Street, comes to a dead end, makes a loop, and runs back to North Chase Street. The origin of this street name was not determined for certain, but the most likely choice would be William Thomas Bryan (1867-1922). Bryan moved to Athens from Union Point as a young man and became successful in a number of business ventures. Some of his many accomplishments included being one of the founders of the Southern Manufacturing Company and serving as president of the Athens Electric Railway Company. Bryan also was a director of the Southern Mutual Insurance Company. The first reference found for this street was in the *Athens Banner*, April 15, 1910. There also was a reference to a Bryant Street in the *Weekly Banner*, February 18, 1910, but this was an error and should have been Bryan Street. The name of the street also was incorrectly identified as Bryant Street in some issues of the *Athens City Directory* in the 1940s and 1950s.

Bryant Street—See **Bryan Street**

Buena Vista Avenue originally ran parallel to Prince Avenue on what is now the western end of Boulevard. Now, slightly reconfigured, the old Buena Vista Avenue was renamed Yonah Avenue. The present Buena Vista Avenue is an entirely different street that runs perpendicular from Prince Avenue and connects with Boulevard. General Robert Taylor (1787-1859) owned a 338-acre farm named Buena Vista on the Federal Road (Prince Avenue) in the 1840s, and this street undoubtedly was named for that farm. The name Buena Vista came from the Mexican town of Buenavista and was popularized by the Mexican War (1846-1848). The Spanish name "Buena Vista" translates to "Good View" in English.

Burnett Avenue probably was named for Wiley Baxter Burnett (1852-1904) because he was the most prominent person with the name Burnett in early Athens. Wiley Burnett was born in Asheville, North Carolina, and came to Athens as a young man. He married Annie R. Jones from Edgefield, South Carolina. Burnett became a lawyer and was a partner with Edwin King Lumpkin in the firm Lumpkin & Burnett. Burnett was a delegate to the national Democratic Convention in 1896 and 1900 and was a member of the Georgia General Assembly. Burnett also served as Athens postmaster during the first term of U.S. President Stephen Grover Cleveland. Burnett was variously referred to in newspaper articles as Capt. Burnett or Col. Burnett. Burnett was a rising star on the political scene when he was cut down by a stroke at only 52 years old. The first reference found for Burnett Avenue was in the 1909 *Athens City Directory*.

Cain Street is a one-block-long, dead-end street that runs west off Lyndon Avenue between Prince Avenue and The Boulevard in the Morristown neighborhood. Cain Street probably was named for John R. Cain (1854-1909), who worked for the City of Athens as "Superintendant of the Street Hands." Cain was very popular and well liked by Athenians. During the latter part of his career, Cain worked under then-Street Commisioner John William Barnett (1868-1962). The first reference found for this street name was in the *Athens Banner*, January 14, 1911. See Morristown in the section on Athens Communities and Neighborhoods.

Carlton Avenue, Carlton Road, Carlton Street, and **Carlton Terrace** probably were all named for Dr. Henry Hull Carlton (1834-1905), perhaps the best known and most beloved member of the Carlton family in Athens. However, Dr. Carlton's father, brothers, and other family members also were prominent and much loved by Athenians, so the various routes bearing this name may have been to honor other family members or perhaps the entire Carlton family. It is noteworthy that in Clarke County Deed Book 81, page 474, Carlton Terrace was identified as being another name for Georgia Factory Road, the early route from Athens to Whitehall.

Athens Streets & Neighborhoods

Carr Street begins at the intersection with Oak Street in East Athens and runs southwest across Georgia Drive and Oconee Street and terminates at the northwest gate to Oconee Hill Cemetery. See Carr's Hill for information regarding the origin of the name. (See Fig. 3 and 4).

Castalia Avenue is a one-block-long street that runs north and south to connect Oakland Avenue and Milledge Circle, one block west of Five Points. The origin of the name of this street is not known, but in Greek mythology Castalia was the name of a nymph who threw herself into a spring to evade the pursuit of the god Apollo. The spring was named for her and became a source of inspiration for Apollo and the Muses. The first mention found of Castalia Avenue was in the [Athens] *Weekly Banner*, December 28, 1900.

Catawba Avenue is a one-block-long street that runs east and west to connect Cherokee Avenue and Highland Avenue. Possibly was named for the Catawba Indians who inhabit North Carolina and South Carolina. The name means "people of the river."

Cemetery Street originally was named Nisbet Street and was an extension of Jackson Street that led from downtown to Oconee Hill Cemetery. This section of steet eventually also was named Jackson Street. Many years ago, the street was diverted slightly to the west to bypass the cemetery instead of leading directly into it and later became present-day East Campus Drive—between the cemetary and the stadium. (See Fig. 15).

Chase Street extends for about 15 blocks from Barber Street at the northern end to Dearing Street at the south, except for one block between Prince Avenue and Cobb Street, which was renamed Prince Place many years ago. (See Prince Place). Chase Street was named for Albon Chase (1808-1867), Athens businessman who was secretary of the Southern Mutual Insurance Company after the company was moved to Athens from Griffin, Georgia. Chase also served one term as Intendant (Mayor) of Athens in 1852. During his time in office, a telegraph line was completed from Athens to Union Point. The first reference found for Chase Street was in the *Southern Watchman*, July 21, 1859. The northern part of this street, from Prince Avenue to Chatooga Avenue, was among several new streets created when the Athens Park and Improvement Company developed this area in the 1890s.

Chattooga Avenue (also Chatooga Avenue) is one of the new streets created when the Athens Park and Improvement Company developed a large tract of land north of Prince Avenue and west of Barber Street in the 1890s. It is one of at least eight streets in the neighborhood that was given an Indian name. The street runs east and west to connect Nacoochee Avenue with Chase Street. The first reference found to the spelling of Chattooga Avenue was in the *Athens Banner* on November 13, 1891. The first reference found for the spelling Chatooga Avenue was in the *Athens Banner* on June 28, 1912. Also see Chatuga Avenue. (See Fig. 11).

Chatuga Avenue is an alternate spelling of Chattooga, but different streets in different parts of Athens have had both these names. Since Chatuga Avenue intersected with Tallulah Avenue, it is speculated that both names derived from Rabun County in Northeast Georgia: the Chatuga (also Chattooga) River and Tallulah Falls. According to an article in the *Athens Daily Herald*, the name of Tallulah Avenue was changed to West View Drive on January 3,

1923. Later, the name of Chatuga Avenue was changed to Woodland Way, a one-block-long, dead-end street that runs southwest off present-day West View Drive (formerly Tallulah Avenue).

Cherry Street was changed to DuBose Avenue. DuBose Avenue is in the Morristown neighborhood and runs east and west for three blocks, connecting Chase Street with Grady Avenue. The first reference found for Cherry Street was in the *Athens Weekly Banner*, March 15, 1892.

Childs Street was named for Asaph King Childs (1820-1902), partner in Childs & Nickerson Hardware. He was involved in numerous other successful business ventures in Athens, including being a founder of the National Bank of Athens in 1866. Childs lived on the corner of Clayton and Thomas streets but later bought the Joseph Henry Lumpkin House on Prince Avenue. Childs Street that now runs beside the property was established and named for Childs after he moved into Lumpkin's former house. This house still stands.

Church Street was named for Alonzo Church, (1793-1862) sixth president of the University of Georgia who served longer than any other UGA president (1829-1859). Church Street runs south from Hill Street, crosses Broad Street and Baxter Street, and terminates at Cloverhurst Avenue. There also was a Church Street located in Oconee Heights. See Oconee Heights in the section on Athens Communities and Neighborhoods for additional information.

Clarkesville Road was changed to "Road to Harmony Grove and Clarkesville." In 1904, the name of the town of Harmony Grove was changed to Commerce, and this route now is locally called

Gary L. Doster

Commerce Road, although its "official" name is U.S. Highway 441 North and/or State Route 15.

Clayton Street was named for Augustin Smith Clayton (1783-1839), circuit judge and one of Athens' most progressive and prominent citizens. Clayton was in the first class that graduated from the University of Georgia in 1804. Clayton and Clayton County, Georgia, also are named for A. S. Clayton. Clayton Street runs east and west for six blocks from Thomas Street to Pulaski Street.

Cleveland Avenue was introduced to the public in a short item on page three of the *Banner-Watchman*, November 11, 1884, titled "New Streets." The article announced that "Col. T. C. Hampton has had his lots surveyed and laid out with broad and beautiful streets and avenues. He has Cleveland Avenue, Hendricks Avenue, Tilden Street, and Gantt Street." Thomas Lawrence "Larry" Gantt (1847-1931), owner and editor of the *Banner-Watchman* at that time, further wrote, "We thank our friend Tom [Hampton] for the honor he has thus conferred upon the Editor of the *Banner-Watchman*, and we will promise never to disgrace the illustrious name of democrats among which we are placed." In addition to naming a street for Larry Gantt, it is obvious that Hampton was a loyal Democrat and also was honoring Stephen Grover Cleveland (1837-1908), who had just won the election for his first term as president of the United States; Thomas Andrews Hendricks (1819-1895), former governor of Indiana and U.S. vice-president under Cleveland from March 4, 1884, until his death nine months later on November 25, 1815; and Samuel Jones Tilden (1814-1886), democratic candidate for U.S. president in 1876 (Tilden actually won the election according to the popular vote, but the office was awarded to Rutherford B. Hayes by the Electoral College because of a supposed discrepancy in the vote count). Athens was staunchly democratic at that time, and Cleveland was extremely popular with Athenians. In his *Annals of Athens Georgia*, A. L. Hull wrote, "A great jubilation was held in Athens over Cleveland's election in 1884." Hull then went on to describe a huge celebration, including music, speeches, and a parade in honor of Cleveland's election. Of Col. Hampton's four new streets he established and named in 1884, Cleveland Avenue and Hendricks Avenue remain. The name of Gantt Street was changed to Tibbetts Street 24 years later at a meeting of the City Council on February 6, 1908. The location and present status of Tilden Street could not be determined.

Clover Street was the original name for Hillcrest Avenue (See Fig. 6), not to be confused with the current Clover Street, a few blocks to the west. On Barnett's 1895 map of Athens, this street was shown to be considerably longer than it actually is. See Bowdre Street for more information on these streets.

Cloverhurst Avenue was named for Cloverhurst Farm, a 200-acre property that fronted on South Milledge Avenue, established by John Armstrong Meeker in the 1870s. Meeker introduced clover to the Athens area as a means of reclaiming worn-out soil, and the name of his farm was derived from that plant. Meeker sold the farm to Dr. Henry Hull Carlton in January 1885 for $15,000. Meeker then moved to Virginia where he died in 1904. Carlton remodeled the existing house on the property, and turned it into a magnificent Second Empire style home. He then also named his new home Cloverhurst. Present-day Cloverhurst Avenue was the driveway to the house. Carlton sold the property to Judge Hamilton McWhorter in 1901 when McWhorter moved his family to Athens from nearby Lexington. After McWhorter's death in

1929, the house was demolished and the land was subdivided and sold.

Cobb Street runs east and west from Prince Avenue to King Avenue and was named for John Addison Cobb (1783-1855), father of Howell Cobb, Sr. and Thomas R. R. Cobb. Cobb and his family came to Athens from Jefferson County, Georgia, in about 1818. Cobb owned and developed a large tract of land off Prince Avenue that comprises the present-day community of Cobbham.

Cohen Street is a one-block-long, dead-end street that runs west off Lyndon Avenue between Prince Avenue and The Boulevard in the Morristown neighborhood. The origin of this street name was not determined for sure, but the most likely individuals for whom it was named are Julius Cohen (1839-1904) or Aaron Cohen (1864-1955). Both were prominent and successful businessmen, and both were active in civic and social organizations. The first reference found for this street was in the *Weekly Banner*, June 9, 1899. See Morristown.

College Avenue was included on this list because it was one of the first streets in Athens and was well known. It begins at the intersection with Broad Street (Front Street) in front of the University of Georgia arch and extends north from there for ten blocks to dead end with Willow Street. No doubt, College Avenue was so named because it was closely associated with Franklin College, the original beginning part of the University of Georgia.

Commerce Road—See **Clarkesville Road**.

Compress Street no doubt was so named because it led to a cotton compress facility where loose ginned cotton was formed into bales. The street has not been located, but in the 1926-27 *Athens City Directory*, it was identified as "going south from Broad Street at the Georgia Railroad crossing." The first reference found for Compress Street was in the *Athens Banner*, January 16, 1910.

Crawford Avenue is a one-block-long, dead-end street that runs south from Cleveland Avenue and is parallel with Barber Street. The first reference found for this street name was in the *Weekly Banner*, January 11, 1907. It is not known for sure for whom this street was named, but it may have been Hiram Hayes Crawford (c.1866-1896), partner in the immensely successful Webb-Crawford Company, a huge wholesale grocery firm that served much of the state of Georgia.

If not for Hiram Hayes Crawford, it would not be unreasonable to assume that the street was named to honor William Harris Crawford (1772-1834) from adjoining Oglethorpe County. Crawford had close ties with Athens, the University of Georgia, and Athens citizens. Crawford was born in Virginia but later moved to South Carolina, then to Columbia County, Georgia. Crawford began practicing law in Lexington, Georgia, in 1799. He was elected to the Georgia House of Representatives in 1803 and became a U.S. senator from Georgia in 1807. Crawford was elected president *pro tempore* of the senate in 1811, and when U.S. Vice-President George Clinton died on April 20, 1812, Crawford became the first acting vice-president and served in that capacity until March 4, 1813. In 1813, President James Madison appointed Crawford as the U.S. minister to France, and Crawford held that post until 1815. President Madison then appointed Crawford as U.S. secretary of war. After slightly more than a year in that office, Crawford became U.S. secretary of the treasury. He remained in that position through the rest of Madison's term, which ended in 1825. William H. Crawford was considered to be a major contender for the U.S. presidency in the 1824 election, running against Andrew Jackson and John Quincy Adams, but a stroke he suffered in 1823 reduced his chances, and Adams was elected. Crawford is buried in a family plot at his old home site near Crawford, Georgia, his namesake.

Dearing Street was named for William Dearing (1785-1853), one of the founders and second president of the Georgia Rail Road and Banking Company. Dearing Street runs east and west for eight blocks from Finley Street to Rocksprings Street.

Devil's Ford Road is a short dead-end road that runs east off Phoenix Road on the property at Whitehall owned by the University of Georgia's Warnell School of Forestry and Natural Resources. The origin of the name was not determined, but it is speculated that long ago it likely led to a ford across the North Oconee River.

Dobbs Street no longer exists, and it is not known where it was located. The only reference found for this street was in the 1920-21 *Athens City Directory*. It may have been named for Burney Springer Dobbs, President of Armstrong & Dobbs or Stephen C. Dobbs (1832-1895), listed in the 1889 *Athens City Directory* as the owner of a grocery at 313 E. Broad Street. In his obituary in the *Semi-Weekly Banner* May 28, 1895, Steven Dobbs was recognized as "...one of the best known and most highly esteemed citizens of Athens..." Dobbs was a member of the City Board of Education, was chairman of the Board of Deacons of First Baptist Church, and was one of the most distinguished Masons in Athens.

Athens Streets & Neighborhoods

Doboy Street no longer exists. It was a three-block-long street that ran south from Baldwin Street about where present-day Sanford Drive dead ends into Baldwin, and it ended at Tanyard Branch on the south side of the present-day Tate Student Center. (See Fig. 9). Some of Athens' most prominent early families had strong ties to Sapelo Island, Georgia, and visited there often. Doboy Sound borders the southern tip of Sapelo Island, and Sapelo Sound is on the northern end. It is probable that Doboy Street was named for Doboy Sound because of the affection these Athenians had for the area. The first reference found for Doboy Street was in the *Banner-Watchman*, May 19, 1889. Also see Sapelo Street.

Dr. Martin Luther King, Jr. Parkway—See **Water Street.**

Dougherty Street no doubt was named for Judge Charles Dougherty (1800-1853), lawyer, legislator, and judge. Dougherty served as president of the Georgia Senate. Dougherty County in south Georgia was named in his honor the year he died. According to Hull's *Annals of Athens, Georgia*, Dougherty Street was known as Walton Street in the early history of Athens.

DuBose Avenue formerly was named Cherry Street. This is a two-block-long street running east and west on the north side of Prince Avenue connecting Grady Avenue and Lyndon Avenue. The origin of the name of this street was not determined for sure, but the most likely member of the DuBose family in Athens to have a street named for him was Robert Toombs DuBose (1859-1929), prominent businessman and 11-term member of the Georgia House of Representatives; DuBose also served one term in the Georgia State Senate. The first reference found for DuBose Avenue was in the *Athens Banner*, December 4, 1907.

Dudley Drive is a one-block-long street that runs north and south to connect Baxter Drive with Fortson Drive and no doubt was named for Alonzo Gordon "Lon" Dudley (1880-1947), prominent and successful Athens businessman who served as mayor of Athens from 1926 to 1935 and 1938 to 1939. Among his many other accomplishments, Dudley founded the Athens Country Club.

East Campus Drive—See **Nisbet Street**.

Elizabeth Street—See **Ruth Street**.

Epps Bridge Road was named for the Epps family who had a farm in this vicinity. There is a small family graveyard in the area where some early members of the Epps Family are buried, including William Epps (1799-1865) and his wife, Sarah Alexander Epps (1802-1852). In 1909, William and Sarah's great-grandson, Benjamin Thomas Epps, Sr. (1888-1937), built and flew the first airplane in Georgia, which also was the first monoplane flown in the United States. Present-day Athens-Ben Epps Airport was started by Ben Epps in 1917.

Erwin Street originally ran off Prince Avenue, parallel with Buena Vista Avenue. Now, slightly reconfigured, the old Buena Vista Avenue was renamed Yonah Avenue. The origin of this street name was not determined for sure, but the most likely candidate is Judge Andrew Smith Erwin (1843-1907). Erwin was married to Mary Ann Lamar Cobb, daughter of Howell Cobb, Sr. and Mary Ann Lamar Cobb. Erwin's wife originated the idea for the Confederate Cross of Honor for the United Daughters of the Confederacy, and Judge Erwin received the first Cross awarded on April 26, 1900.

Athens Streets & Neighborhoods

Espy Street no longer exists, but the description in the 1859 Street Committee list says the street extended "...from junction of Lumpkin St. with Milledge Avenue [and continued] on by Dr. Church's place." The origin of the name is undetermined, but the street likely was named for one or both of the Espy twins, James and John. The name also is seen spelled as Espey. James and John were identified by Hull in *Annals of Athens, Georgia* as Revolutionary War veterans who were "...excellent men and citizens of blameless, useful lives and irreproachable character." James and John were further identified by Hull as faithful Presbyterians who helped found Sandy Creek Church in northern Clarke County, the forerunner of First Presbyterian Church in Athens, at which both served as Ruling Elders. James Espy's obituary on page three of the November 15, 1834, issue of the *Southern Banner* also identified him as serving in the army during the Revolutionary War and stated that earlier in his life he lived in Oglethorpe County and represented the county in the Georgia General Assembly. James is buried in the Old Athens Cemetery on Jackson Street. John Espy's gravesite is unknown, but current descendants believe he is also buried in the Old Athens Cemetery on Jackson Street.

Factory Street was present-day **Mitchell Street**. According to the 1859 street committee's list, Factory Street was identified as "...beginning at Broad Street between [the] Banner office and Bernardos by the town spring and African Baptist Church to Factory." The Factory was the Athens Factory (later Athens Manufacturing Company) located on present-day Williams Street. At this writing, the University of Georgia's School of Social Work is housed in part of the old Athens Manufacturing Company building.

Federal Road, The — See **Prince Avenue**.

Ferdinand Street no longer exists by that name, but it appears to have been the west end of present-day Morton Avenue as it leaves South Milledge Avenue. See Phinizy Street for information on the possible origin of the name for Ferdinand Street.

Finley Street was named for Dr. Robert Finley (1769-1817), who came here with his family from New Jersey to accept the position of fourth president of the University of Georgia. Immediately after his arrival, he travelled around the state to collect money to support a library for the university but became sick and died of fever before exercising his duties as president. Virtually all references that record Dr. Finley's name do so with the spelling Finley. However, the street named for him is variously spelled as Finley, Findley, and Findly. The first reference found for the spelling Finley Street appeared in the *Southern Watchman*, December 30, 1868. The first reference found for the spelling of Findley Street was in the *Weekly Banner-Watchman*, December 14, 1886. The first reference found regarding the spelling of Findly Street was in the [Athens] *Weekly Banner*, September 2, 1898.

Flint Street formerly was a two-block-long street in northeast Athens connecting Third Street and Fourth Street. Now, it is a one-block-long street connecting Third Street and Odd Street. The origin of this street name was not determined. The first reference found for this street name was in the *Weekly Banner*, May 2, 1893.

Florida Avenue formerly was named Becker Street. Florida Avenue goes south off West Broad Street, across Waddell Street to Hull Street.

Forbstein Alley also has been seen as Farbstein, Farbtein, and Forestein. This is a short, one-block-long street between Augusta Avenue and Macon Avenue in Newtown (or New Town). The origin of the name of this street was not determined, but the only Athenians discovered with one of these names was the Farbstein family, so it is assumed that the street was named for a member of that family.

Fortson Drive connects West Lake Drive with Bobbin Mill Road. The street likely was named for Superior Court Judge Blanton Erwin Fortson, Sr. (1882-1968). Fortson was born in Washington, Georgia, but moved to Athens as a young man and remained here for the rest of his life. Blanton served as Superior Court Judge for the Western Judicial Circuit from 1921 to 1940. The first reference found for this street was in the *Athens Banner* December 12, 1916.

Foundry Street was identified by the 1859 committee for naming streets as going "From East end of Broad running north by the Foundry to the river." The foundry referred to the Athens Foundry and Machine Works, formerly Athens Steam Company.

Fowler Avenue no longer exists. It was located on the east side of South Lumpkin Street between present-day Smith Street and East Rutherford Street. The first reference found for this street was in the *Weekly Banner*, June 21, 1901.

Franklin Street was named for Leonidas Franklin (c.1810-1867), who was an early resident of Athens. The original Franklin Street was five-blocks-long and ran north from Reese Street to Prince Avenue. Present-day Franklin Street covers this same route, but has another one-block-long leg south of the main route that runs north from Fuller Street to Dearing Street.

Front Street—see **Broad Street**.

Fuller Street runs south from Waddell Street to Henderson Extension. The origin of this street name was not determined. The first reference found for Fuller Street was in the *Weekly Banner*, September 12, 1913.

Fulton Street probably was named for James Fulton, who operated a boy's school on the University of Georgia campus about where Fulton Street intersects Jackson Street. In his *Annals of Athens*, Hull wrote: "Mr. James Fulton taught a boy's school near the Bishop residence on Jackson Street. He was a strict disciplinarian and believed in a free use of the birch. There are still among us some of his old pupils who have a feeling recollection of his attentions." The 1859 list of Athens streets said the street went "from Jackson Street between Mr. Terry's back of Granite row to Thomas St." (See Fig. 14).

Gantt Street was established in November 1884 and was named for Thomas Lawrence "Larry" Gantt (1847-1931), owner and editor of the *Athens Banner-Watchman* at that time. The name was changed to Tibbetts Street on February 6, 1908. This is a one-block-long street that runs west off Pulaski Street and connects with Hendricks Avenue. Also see Cleveland Avenue and Tibbetts Avenue.

Georgia Depot Street—See **Georgia Drive**.

Georgia Drive formerly was named Georgia Depot Street. This street covers the old track bed for the Georgia Rail Road that came into Athens in 1840. As it approached Athens from the East, the train track crossed present-day Oak Street and went the length of what later was named Georgia Depot Street to the depot near the intersection with Oconee Street. The train track was rerouted in 1882 and the old track bed was converted to the street. Discussions for paving Georgia Depot Street began in the Athens Mayor and Council Meetings as early as September 1948 but it was not until 1955 that the street was widened and paved at the request of the residents along the street. A petition dated October 1, 1957, requesting that the name be changed to Georgia Drive, was signed by all 16 property owners on the street, and the name was so changed. (See Fig. 4).

Georgia Factory Road originally turned off the end of South Milledge Avenue, as shown on W. W. Thomas' 1874 Map of Athens. (See Fig. 2). This was the road that led from Athens to the community of Whitehall, the location of John White's Georgia Factory. It is noteworthy that in Clarke County Deed Book 81, page 474, Carlton Terrace was identified as being another name for Georgia Factory Road.

Gilleland Drive is a two-block-long street that runs south off Oglethorpe Avenue and terminates where Lucille Street begins. The street was named for John Wesley Gilleland, Sr. (1808-1875), a local carpenter and member of the Mitchell Thunderbolts, who was the originator of the famous double-barreled cannon that now sits on the lawn of the Athens City Hall. Gilleland proposed that two cannon balls could be connected with a chain and fired simultaneously from the two barrels, which diverged about three degrees, and that when they left the gun they would separate, draw the chain tight, and mow down large numbers of the enemy. Unfortunately, the gun could not be made to fire both barrels at the same time, and the gun was deemed a failure. On January 12, 1912, Dr. William Buchanan Conway (1845-1920) conducted an interview with Thomas Bailey, who worked at the Athens Foundry & Machine Works where the double-barreled cannon was made in 1863. In his affidavit, Thomas Bailey said that he was on the scene when the cannon was made and assisted with its creation (this affidavit was donated to the Hargrett Library by Patrick Mizelle, a great-grandson of William Buchanan Conway). Bailey said that John Gilleland raised $350 in Confederate money from local citizens to finance the building of the cannon and had Mr. W. A. Bain make the patterns. The patterns were turned over to a "Mr. Tweety," who was the foreman of the foundry and supervised the casting of the gun. Bailey further testified that there were several workmen at the foundry who participated in its manufacture, including Jonathan Garwood. The first cannon cast was a failure, and a second one was made. It was sent to the machine shop and the barrels were bored out by a "Mr. Little." Thomas Bailey drew the plans for the touch holes and bored them out himself. Bailey said the site for the trial firing was at "Dr. Linton's lot on Barber Street near his old residence." Bailey identified Jeff Bridges as the individual who test fired the cannon. At the same time the affidavit was secured from Thomas Bailey, a petition was delivered to Athens mayor H. J. Rowe requesting that a plate be placed on the cannon identifying John W. Gilleland as the maker. The petition was signed by committee chairman Dr. William Buchanan Conway and committee members John Emmeus Talmadge, Sr. and Thomas Howard Dozier, Sr.

Gilmer Street was a one-block-long street that ran east and west and connected South Hull Street with South Lumpkin Street. The name was later changed to White Street. The street was abolished in modern times to allow for expansion of the Holiday Inn. There is a present-day Gilmer Street that is one block long and runs east and west to connect Hawthorne Avenue and Oaktree Street. There were no prominent Gilmers in Athens in earlier times, and it is probable that this street was named for Georgia Governor George Rockingham Gilmer (1790-1859) from adjoining Oglethorpe County. Gilmer was a friend and supporter of the University of Georgia.

Glenhaven Avenue—See **Bowdre Street**.

Grace Street was a two-block-long street that ran east and west between College Avenue and the North Oconee River. This street no longer exists. The origin of this street name was not determined. The first reference found for this street was in the *Weekly Banner-Watchman*, July 20, 1886.

Grady Avenue is a two-block-long street that runs north and south to connect Prince Avenue with Boulevard. The street borders the property occupied by the Taylor-Grady House. Rowe (1923) said this street was named for William Sammons Grady (1821-1864), father of Henry Woodfin Grady (1850-1889), but it could have been named for either of them or both of them. William S. Grady was a business partner with his brother-in-law John William Nicholson (1824-1886). Grady and Nicholson established the first gas works in Athens, providing gas lights for the streets, businesses, and private homes. In 1863, William S. Grady bought the Richard Deloney Bolling Taylor house on Prince Avenue that now is known as the Taylor-Grady House. Shortly thereafter, William S. Grady was killed during the War Between the States without ever having lived in the house. His son Henry Grady became a famous journalist before his short life was ended at age 39. A famous hospital in Atlanta is named for him, as well as the University of Georgia's School of Journalism. The first reference found for this street name was in the *Weekly Banner*, August 11, 1894.

Gran Ellen Drive is one of the "newer" Athens streets included in this essay because the origin of the name is known, and we want to preserve the information for future historians. The street name was derived from the first name of the man who developed this neighborhood in the late 1940s, Grandison Marion Caskey, Jr., and the middle name of his wife, Laura Ellen Jordan Caskey. The street runs southwest from South Milledge Avenue, through Memorial Park, to South Lumpkin Street. The first reference found for Gran Ellen Drive was in the 1949 *Athens, Georgia, City Directory*. Most of this information on Gran Ellen Drive was obtained via personal communication with Nancy Bowen, who has conducted considerable research on the G.M. Caskey family. Also see Marion Drive.

Graveyard Street originally was named Brown Street, then Graveyard Street, before becoming Magazine Street. This was a one-block-long street that ran along the northern boundary of the Old Athens Cemetery on Jackson Street and connected South Jackson Street with South Thomas Street (See Fig. 8). The street was obliterated when the UGA Visual Arts Building (now the College of Environmental Design) was constructed on Jackson Street.

Green Street was an early name for Hancock Avenue. The origin of the name of Green Street was not determined for certain, but it may have been named for University of Georgia mathmatics professor Dr. William Green. He began teaching at UGA in 1813 and was asked to resign in 1816 at the same time UGA president John Brown resigned over difficulties with the Board of Trustees. In addition to being a UGA professor, Green is reputed to have been a leader in the failed Irish revolution of 1799. According to Henry Hull in A. L. Hull's *Annals of Athens, Georgia*, during the War of 1812, Dr. Green was put in charge of the defense of Athens when it was feared that a band of Indians would attack the town. After leaving UGA, William Green became a newspaper editor.

Griffith Street is a one-block-long street that runs from Third Street to Odd Street in East Athens. The origin of this street name was not determined.

Habersham Street appears on W. W. Thomas' 1874 map of Athens along with Adams Street as the only two streets named in a new subdivision on Milledge Avenue between present-day Rutherford Street and Five Points. (See Fig. 2). The subdivision was called "Adams Estate." Adams Street probably was named for one-term Athens Mayor, Flournoy Woodbridge "Ferdy" Adams, and Habersham Street probably was named for his brother, Habersham J. Adams (1827-1898). Habersham's first wife was Flora N. Williamson; he later married Florida "Florrie" Virginia Wilkerson (1837-1886). In the mid-1800s Habersham Adams was a member of the firm of Lampkin & Adams and they published the *Southern Herald* newspaper about 1849 or 1850. Adams then entered the jewelry business with Asaph King Childs for a while. In 1856, Adams united with the Georgia Methodist Conference and became a Methodist preacher. Habersham J. Adams died in

St. Louis, Missouri, in 1898. Habersham Street no longer exists by that name, but it appears to have been where present-day Oakland Avenue is located. Also see Adams Street. The first reference found for Habersham Street was in the *Athens Banner*, January 6, 1910.

Hall Street used to be a two-block-long street that ran east off Bloomfield Street, crossed Church Street, and continued to Cloverhurst Avenue. Now, the street comes to a dead end between Church Street and Cloverhurst Avenue. The origin of this street name was not determined. The first reference found for this street name was in the *Athens Banner*, May 28, 1913.

Hampton Avenue now is called Hampton Court and runs east and west from South Milledge Avenue to D. W. Brooks Drive. The street probably was named for T. C. Hampton. The first reference found for Hampton Avenue was in the June 11, 1909, issue of *The Athens Banner*. The first reference found for Hampton Court was in the July 26, 1915, issue of *The Athens Daily Herald*.

Hancock Avenue was named for Thomas Hancock (1771-1852), who moved to Athens from Jefferson County, Georgia, in 1819. Hancock's home on the corner of Hancock Avenue and Lumpkin Street served as a stagecoach stop, hotel, and tavern. The VonCannon-Wall Building now occupies the site. In a deed dated November 8, 1824, Mr. Hancock donated the land where the First Methodist Church now stands. The deed stipulated that the church had to be built within two years or the land would revert to Hancock; it was completed the next year in 1825. According to Hull's *Annals of Athens*, in the early history of Athens, Hancock Avenue was originally named Green Street.

Athens Streets & Neighborhoods

Harper Street is a one-block-long street in East Athens that used to run southwest from Herring Street to Branch Street. Now that part of Branch Street no longer exists, so Harper Street now is a dead-end street. The origin of this street name was not determined. The first reference found for Harper Street was in the 1897-98 Athens City Directory.

Harris Street begins at Prince Avenue and runs south, parallel with Milledge Avenue, crosses Broad Street and Baxter Street and ends at Peabody Street. Rowe (1923) said this street was named for either Jeptha Vining Harris (1782-1856) or Stephen Willis Harris (?-1822). Drewry (1963) attributed the street name to Jeptha Vining Harris. Reed (1948) believed that the street was named for Young Loftin Gerdine Harris (1812-1894).

Jeptha Harris was born in Wilkes County, Georgia. He was in the first class to graduate from the University of Georgia in 1804 and graduated with the highest honors. Jeptha V. Harris was a brigadier general in the Georgia militia during the War of 1812. Harris was a lawyer and plantation owner and served as both a Georgia state representative and Georgia state senator. He also was a trustee of the University of Georgia from 1832 to 1856. Harris practiced law in Athens for many years. General Harris died at his home in Cobb County, Georgia, June 29, 1856, and was buried in Old Madison Cemetery in Madison, Georgia.

Stephen W. Harris lived where St. Mary's Hospital stood at 360 North Milledge Avenue. The old hospital building was vacated in 1966 and was demolished in the early 1970s. The lot remained vacant for many years. The lot is now occupied by Gastroenterology Associates of Athens.

Young L. G. Harris was president of the Southern Mutual Insurance Company for fifty years, served on the UGA Board of

Trustees, and was one of the founders of Young Harris College. The college and the town of Young Harris, Georgia, were named for him, as was Young Harris Memorial United Methodist Church in Athens.

Hart Avenue is a one-block-long street that connects King Avenue with the southern end of Hodgson Drive, just before it enters West Broad Street. The street could have been named for Nancy Hart, heroine of the Revolutionary War, for whom Hart County and Hartwell, Georgia, are named, but this is not known for sure. If so, this would be one of the few Athens streets known to be named for a woman.

Helen Street was in the same neighborhood with Olivia Street and Marion Street. (See Fig. 7). All three streets ran off Carlton Avenue on the west side of South Milledge Avenue, directly behind "Cloverhurst," the home of Dr. Henry Hull Carlton (1834-1905) and his wife, Helen Camak Newton Carlton (1844-1934). It is obvious that Helen Street, Marion Street, and Olivia Street were named for the daughters of H. H. and Helen Carlton; the three girls were the granddaughters of John Hamlin Newton (1800-1889) and Mary Jordan Newton (1904-1893). It is not certain that any of these streets ever existed other than on Barnett's 1895 map of Athens, except that Olivia Street may be the present site of Rutherford Street.

Henderson Avenue originally was named States' Rights Street (See Fig. 5). Henderson Avenue was aptly named for Dr. Matthew Henry Henderson (?-1872), rector of Emmanuel Church for many years who was beloved by all who knew him. The first reference found for the name States' Rights Street was in the *Athens*

Banner, January 25, 1881. The first reference found for the name Henderson Avenue was in the *Athens Daily Banner*, September 28, 1897, when it was announced that the name had been changed from States' Rights Street.

Hendricks Avenue is a one-block-long, dead-end street that runs south from Cleveland Avenue and ends at the railroad tracks. (See Fig. 10). The street was named for Thomas Andrews Hendricks (1819-1885), former governor of Indiana and U.S. vice-president under President Grover Cleveland from March 4, 1884, until his death nine months later on November 25, 1885. Also see Cleveland Avenue.

Herring Street is a two-block-long street in East Athens that runs east and west to connect Peter Street and Derby Street. It is quite likely that the street was named for John Newton Herring who lived on Herring Street. Herring was a lifelong employee of the Athens Manufacturing Company and in charge of the wool department at the factory for eight years before he died. Herring was a member of St. Marys Episcopal Church and was a member of the Odd Fellows fraternal organization. Several members of Herring's family are buried in the Factory Burying Ground in Oconee Hill Cemetery, and it is likely that John Herring also is buried there. The first reference found for Herring Street was when John Herring's obituary was published in the *Athens Weekly Banner*, January 26, 1892.

Herty Drive used to run south from Broad Street to Baldwin Street, parallel with Jackson Street. Only remnants of the north end and south end are left; a large portion of the central part of the street now is occupied by Herty Field, a large public plaza with a fountain. The street and the park were named for Dr. Charles Holmes Herty (1867-1938), a University of Georgia chemistry professor who brought football and other intercollegiate sports to UGA. Although Dr. Herty is remembered by most for his athlethic interests, he also was world famous for his scientific skills, including developing the process of making paper from pine tree pulp.

Hiawassee Avenue is one of the new streets created when the Athens Park and Improvement Company developed a large tract of land north of Prince Avenue and west of Barber Street in the 1890s. (See Fig. 11). This is one of at least eight streets in the neighborhood that was given an Indian name. The name Hiawassee comes from the Cherokee Indian word *Ayuhwasi*, which means meadow. The first reference found for Hiawassee Avenue was in the *Weekly Banner* on November 22, 1895.

Hill Street runs east and west from Prince Avenue to King Avenue. Newcomers and native Athenians alike often assume that this street was named for Senator Benjamin Harvey Hill (1823-1882), who lived in Athens and was quite famous in his day. Senator Hill was an earlier owner of the UGA president's house on Prince Avenue. However, Rowe (1923) said this street was named for Blanton Meade Hill (1802-1857), successful Athens merchant, whose house occupied the corner of Pulaski Street and Hancock Avenue where First Baptist Church now stands.

Hillcrest Avenue was first named Clover Street (See Fig. 6), not to be confused with present-day Clover Street, a few blocks to the west. This street is included on Barnett's 1895 map of Athens, but it does not comport with Barnett's depiction of the street on that map. Hillcrest Avenue extends southwest from Cobb Street for three blocks then connects with Brookwood Drive.

Hobson Avenue used to be the name of present-day Dr. Martin Luther King, Jr. Parkway from the intersection of Water Street and Strickland Street to the Athens city limits, but Hobson Avenue now is just a very short street off the Parkway. At the city limits, the route becomes Commerce Road (Highway 441/15 North). The origin of this street name was not determined. The first reference found for Hobson Avenue was in the *Weekly Banner*, July 2, 1909.

Hodgson Avenue originally was named Stewart Street. It was a one-block-long street that connected Clover Street (King Avenue) and Meigs Street (The Plaza). The origin of the name probably is the same as Hodgson Street. The first reference found for Hodgson Avenue was in the *Weekly Banner*, Sept. 5, 1902. (See Fig. 6)

Hodgson Drive runs south from King Avenue to Broad Street. No doubt the name of this street has the same origin as Hodgson Avenue and Hodgson Street.

Hodgson Street was a one-block-long street that connected Strong Street to Bridge Street leading to the bridge on the west side of the North Oconee River. The name was changed to Berry Street on February 6, 1908, but the street no longer exists. There have been a number of prominent members of the Hodgson Family in Athens, many of whom were deserving of having a street named for them, but the most likely candidate is Asbury Hull Hodgson (1850-1913), two-term Athens mayor (1887-1888). The first electric street lights in Athens were installed during Hodgson's service as mayor. Also see Berry Street. The first reference found for Hodgson Street was in the *Athens Weekly Banner*, July 23, 1889.

Holman Avenue was a one-block-long street that connected "old" Clover Street (King Avenue) and Phinizy Street (Hancock Avenue). The original name for the southeast end of this street was Jacob Street. Holman Avenue undoubtedly was named for William Shrewsbury Holman (1844-1931) who built his mansion on Oglethorpe Avenue across the street from the intersection with the northwestern end of Holman Avenue (See Fig. 22). Holman was born in Bowling Green, Kentucky. He came through Athens during the War Between the States and liked the town so much that he came back after the war and spent the rest of his life here. He was involved in many business ventures and was a successful businessman. In 1913, Holman built a nine-story office building on the corner of Clayton Street and Lumpkin Street that later was converted to the Holman Hotel. In the 1960s, the building was renovated to become the C & S Bank, now Bank of America.

Hoyt Street was named for Dr. Nathan Hoyt (1793-1866), minister of the Presbyterian Church for 36 years. The first reference found for Hoyt Street was in an Athens newspaper dated April 23, 1873.

Hughes Avenue ran northwest off Barrett Street (now Ruth Street), parallel with Russell Avenue. Hughes Avenue and Russell Avenue no longer exist. The origin of the name of Hughes Avenue is not known.

Hull Street runs south from Hoyt Street, across Dougherty Street and Broad Street to Baxter Street. Rowe (1923) said this street was named for Asbury Hull (1797-1866), first president of the Southern Mutual Insurance Company after the business was moved to Athens from Griffin, Georgia. Hull built a house on present-day Hull Street that Rowe claimed "…there is none in Athens and few in the state that are more handsome." In later years, this house became known as the Hull-Snelling House at 198 South Hull Street. The house eventually was demolished and the property was paved as a parking lot for the Holiday Inn across the street.

Ingle Street—See **Inglewood Avenue**.

Inglewood Avenue is a two-block-long, dead-end street the runs northeast off Oak Street in East Athens. On a 1952 map of Athens prepared by Jack Beacham and printed by the McGregor Company, it is identified as Ingle Street but no other reference to this name has been found. This street no doubt was named for J. W. Ingle, one of the founders of White City Manufacturing Company in 1909, which was located on Inglewood Avenue and whose business was manufacturing thread and yarn. Apparently, the builders of the mill cut this street through their property to their business for the use and convenience of themselves and their employees. In 1916, the citizens of East Athens petitioned the Mayor and City Council to request that the city improve and maintain the street, saying that it was almost impassable. According to the Minutes of the Mayor and City Council at a meeting on August 25, 1916, "the matter was referred to the Street Commission, the City Engineer, and the City Attorney, with the view of accepting the street when properly laid off and dedicated to the city." Apparently, soon after this meeting these provisions were met and the city accepted ownership of the street and began maintenance on it. For additional information, see White City in the section on Athens Communities and Neighborhoods.

Jackson Street runs south from Madison Avenue across Dougherty Street and Broad Street to Baldwin Street. (See Fig. 8). Rowe (1923) said this street was named for Dr. Henry Jackson (1778-1840), University of Georgia professor, who was the brother of Georgia governor James Jackson and the father of Confederate general Henry Rootes Jackson. Reed (1948) speculated that the street probably was named for General/President Andrew Jackson but also allowed that it may have been named for Dr. Henry Jackson, as most others believed. The first reference found for Jackson Street was in the *Southern Banner*, February 5, 1835, which was during Jackson's presidency and before he died.

Jacob Street is shown on Barnett's 1895 map of Athens as a one-block-long street that connected "old" Clover Street (present-day Hillcrest Avenue) with the southwest end of Phinizy Street (present-day Hancock Avenue). This street apparently never existed except on Barnett's map, and it is thought that it was one of several Athens streets that were named for members of the Phinizy Family. Also see Barrett, Bowdre, Leonard, Phinizy, and Stewart streets. (See Fig. 6).

Jennings Mill Road runs south off the western part of the Atlanta Highway/Highway 78, just before it crosses the Athens Loop. The road crosses McNutt Creek, which is the Clarke/Oconee County boundary line, and continues into Oconee County. The road was named for the Jennings family, who operated a grist mill on McNutt Creek. The family was unusually long-lived for that time and was composed of Henry Jennings (1790-1862), his wife

Nancy Bell Landrum Jennings (1803-1888), and their 12 children: Frances America Jennings Matthews (1821-1909), James Jackson Jennings (1822-1914), Jefferson Jennings (1824-1912), Henrietta Virginia Jennings Daniell (1827-1907), Prudence Elizabeth Jennings Sikes (1829-1903), Matilda Mozelle Jennings Breedlove (1832-1922), Cecilia Penelope Jennings Epps (1834-1895), Cynthia Ann Jennings Langford (1836-1916), Henry Jennings (1839-1916), Nancy Jennings Davenport (1841-1940), Susan Mayne Jennings Reynolds (1843-1913), and Giles Robert Jennings (1846-1927). One of the Jennings sons, Jefferson Jennings, served as a Justice of the Inferior Court of Clarke County, and was elected to be a delegate from Clarke County at the Georgia Secession Convention held in Milledgeville, along with Asbury Hull and T. R. R. Cobb. The Ordinance of Secession, taking Georgia out of the Union, was passed January 19, 1861.

Johns Street now is named John Street. The origin of this street name was not determined. It is a one-block-long street that runs northwest from Third Street to Odd Street in East Athens.

Jonas Avenue is a one-block-long, dead-end street that runs east off Ruth Street. The origin of this street name was not determined.

King Avenue was first identified at a meeting of the Athens City Council on July 23, 1915, when it was announced that King Avenue was a new street and that "...Capt Barnett has laid off the street, fixing the proper permanent grades. The new street will extend from Cobb to Holman Avenue." The steet no longer terminates at Holman Avenue but now crosses Holman and Old Broad Street and dead ends into West Broad Street. This street probably was named for either of two successful and prominent Athenians,

James Sebastian King (1842-1908) or Dr. William C. King (1831-1917).

James S. King was born in North Carolina and came to Athens in 1865 or 1866. He married Sarah C. Boggs (1846-1919) and became a successful merchant. He owned J. S. King and Company, a large wholesale and retail grocery enterprise on the corner of Broad and Thomas streets. In October 1897, King moved his business across the street into the new triangular building between Broad Street and Oconee Street and expanded his business. This building later was the home of Farmers Hardware for many years. In conection with the business affairs of the city, James King was active in the Athens Chamber of Commerce. On two occassions he represented the Chamber at annual meetings of the Southern Cotton Association held in New Orleans. In addition to his business interests, King was concerned with education and was a member of the local Board of Education. James King was so highly regarded by Athenians that on the occasion of his death the City Council appointed a committee to draft a resolution lamenting his death, and Mayor Dorsey announced that all city departments would be closed during his funeral.

On September 3, 1897, James and Sarah King had bought what is now known as the Sledge-Cobb-Spalding House at 749 Cobb Street. At that time, the property consisted of just over 25 acres. When King Avenue was opened in 1915 it came through their property on the western side of their house, which caused their house to be located on the corner of Cobb Street and King Avenue. Although King Avenue was not finished until 1915, seven years after James King's death, the minutes of the Athens City Council show that it was first discussed in a council meeting on December 10, 1908, just six months after his death. At another meeting of the council on June 10, 1909, the Street Committee gave a progress report on the street, which they began calling King Street. The new street was to extend from Cobb Street to the [Old] Epps Bridge Road. The Street Committee gave regular progress reports on King Street until it was finally finished in mid-1915.

If King Avenue was not named for James S. King, the next most likely individual that it was named for would be Dr. William King, former Athens mayor. William King was born in South Carolina but came to Athens at a young age. He graduated from the University of Georgia in 1850 then attended medical school in Philadelphia and returned to Athens to practice medicine for more than twenty years. Dr. King also owned a drug store in Athens for several years, which he eventually sold to Dr. Edward Smith Lyndon. King was married to Augusta Columbiana Clayton (1822-1915), daughter of Augustin Smith Clayton. William and Sarah's daughter Julia married Henry W. Grady. King was twice elected mayor of Athens, in 1874 and 1875 and was renowned for opening and improving many Athens streets during his tenure. William and Augusta King later moved to Atlanta, then, in their old age they moved to Augusta to be near their daughter. Augusta Clayton King died in 1915, but William lived another two years and died in 1917.

LeConte Avenue no doubt was named for brothers James and John LeConte, who were professors at the University of Georgia in the 1850s. Both taught science courses and both were considered to be fine teachers. The original LeConte Hall on the University of Georgia campus was named for the brothers, but the name later was changed to Meigs Hall. Still later, another building, Science Hall, was renamed LeConte Hall and presently houses the UGA History Department.

Lenoir Avenue is one of the streets created when the Athens Park and Improvement Company developed a large tract of land north of Prince Avenue and west of Barber Street in the 1890s. (See Fig. 11). The origin of this street name is unknown. The first reference found for Lenoir Avenue was in the *Weekly Banner*, November 6, 1896. This street originally extended two blocks from Hiawassee, across Nacoochee, to Chase Street. However, when Chase Street School was built in 1922-23, the street was stopped at Nacoochee to become a one-block-long street.

Leonard Street is shown on Barnett's 1895 map of Athens as a one-block-long street that connected "old" Clover Street (present-day Hillcrest Avenue) (See Fig. 6) with the southwest end of Phinizy Street (present-day Hancock Avenue). This street apparently never existed, and it is thought that it was one of several Athens streets named for members of the Phinizy Family. Also see Barrett, Bowdre, Jacob, Phinizy, and Stewart streets.

Long Avenue ran west from Madison Avenue/North Avenue/River Street across Barrett Street (now Ruth Street), parallel with Woods Avenue and Stonewall Avenue. Woods Avenue and Stonewall Avenue no longer exist. Although it has not been documented, surely Long Avenue was named for Dr. Crawford Williamson Long (1815-1878), the discoverer of the use of sulfuric ether as an anesthetic. Dr. Long had a practice in Athens with his brother Dr. Henry Russell Jones Long (1823-1888), and they owned and operated a drug store on Broad Street.

Lumpkin Street has been called Princeton Road, Princeton Factory Road, and Watkinsville Road. Athens has had other famous members of the Lumpkin family, but Rowe (1923) claimed this street was named for Wilson Lumpkin (1783-1870), who was a Georgia legislator, U.S. senator, trustee of the University of Georgia, governor of Georgia, and commissioner to the Cherokee Indians. His granite mansion still stands on Cedar Street on the UGA campus near the intersection with D. W. Brooks Drive. Lumpkin, Georgia, and Lumpkin County, Georgia, also were named for him.

Lyndon Avenue formerly was named Morris Street. This street runs north off Prince Avenue across DuBose Avenue to The Boulevard in the Morristown neighborhood. Undoubtedly, this street's present name was to honor Dr. Edward Smith Lyndon (1839-1917), who moved here from Newnan, Georgia, and bought Dr. William Smith's drug store. Lyndon also practiced medicine but soon retired from that and continued to operate the drug store. Lyndon also bought the home of Dr. Edward Roswell Ware (1803-1873), which remains well known today as the Ware-Lyndon House. The house currently is owned by Athens-Clarke County and houses the Lyndon House Arts Center. The first reference found for Lyndon Avenue was in the *Weekly Banner*, March 10, 1905. Also see Morris Street and Morristown. (See Fig. 11).

Lyndon Row is a two-block-long street that runs east off Church Street to Newton Street. It is assumed that the origin of this name is the same as Lyndon Avenue.

Madison Avenue originally began at College Avenue and ran east across Jackson Street and Thomas Street, then bent northeast to cross the North Oconee River. After crossing the river, Madison Avenue continued to the city limits of Athens where the name changed to Danielsville Road. Eventually, that part of Madison

Avenue across the river became known as River Street, then Water Street, and now is named North Avenue. All that remains of Madison Avenue today is the two-block-long section between College Avenue and Thomas Street. The origin of the name of this street has not been determined, but it may have been named for James Madison (1751-1836), fourth president of the United States.

Magazine Street originally was named Brown Street, then Graveyard Street, before becoming Magazine Street. This was a one-block-long street that ran along the northern boundary of the Old Athens Cemetery on Jackson Street and connected South Jackson Street with South Thomas Street. (See Fig. 8). The street was obliterated when the university's Visual Arts Building (now the College of Environmental Design) was constructed on Jackson Street.

At one time, this street led to a powder magazine in which gun powder, dynamite, nitroglycerine, and other explosives were stored for local merchants in order to isolate them from downtown, hence the reason for the street's name. We know from an article in the *Southern Watchman* that the Athens powder magazine existed as early as October 18, 1855. Merchants were not allowed to keep large quantities of explosives in their place of business and were required to pay the city to store it away from downtown. In the 1880s, the charge for storing powder was one cent per pound per year, and half a cent per pound for each additional six months or less (*Compilation of the Constitutional Provisions and Acts of the Legislature Incorporating and Relating to the City of Athens and Codification of the Ordinances of Said City*. Published by the *Southern Watchman Book and Job Office*, 1881, pp. 26-27). The original location of the powder magazine was not determined, but in 1886 the city planned to build a new one in the Old Athens Cemetery on Jackson Street but complaints from Athens citizens resulted in a change of plans (*Weekly Banner-Watchman*, October 5, 1886). Instead, the new powder magazine was built in the vicinity of the Seaboard Airline Railroad depot at the intersection of Thomas Street and Mitchell Street, about where the UGA Staff Training and Development Building is now situated. In the meeting of the Athens City Council on September 9, 1912, a communication was read from the DuPont Powder Company requesting that the city powder magazine be removed farther from the railroad. The first reference found for Magazine Street was in the *Weekly Banner*, October 20, 1891.

Marion Drive is one of Athens' more "modern" streets. This two-block-long street runs from Gran Ellen Drive on the south to Carlton Terrace to the north. It was named for Grandison Marion Caskey, III, the son of Grandison Marion Caskey, Jr. and Laura Ellen Jordan Caskey, who developed the neighborhood where the street is located. Young Marion Caskey was killed in an automobile accident on January 8, 1953, at age 17. Most of this information was obtained via personal communication with Nancy Bowen, who has conducted considerable research on the G.M. Caskey family. Also see Gran Ellen Drive.

Marion Street was in the same neighborhood with Helen Street and Olivia Street. (See Fig. 7). All three streets ran off Carlton Avenue on the west side of South Milledge Avenue, directly behind Cloverhurst, the home of Dr. Henry Hull Carlton (1834-1905) and his wife, Helen Camak Newton Carlton (1844-1934). It is obvious that Helen Street, Marion Street, and Olivia Street were named for the daughters of H. H. and Helen Carlton; the three girls were the granddaughters of John Hamlin Newton (1800-1889) and Mary Jordan Newton (1904-1893). It is not certain that any of these streets actually existed other than on Barnett's 1895 Map of Athens, except that Olivia Street may be the present site of Rutherford Street.

Marlin Street is a one-block-long, dead-end street that runs north off Strickland Street between Dr. Martin Luther King, Jr. Parkway and North Avenue. The origin of this street name was not determined. The first reference found for Marlin Street was in the 1920-21 *Athens City Directory*.

Market Street—See **Washington Street**.

Matthews Avenue originally was named Bowdre Street. (See Fig. 6). This was a one-block-long street that connected "old" Clover Street (present-day Hillcrest Avenue) with Meigs Street (present-day Glenhaven Avenue). The origin of the name was not determined.

McWhorter Street is in two separate sections. One part runs south from Cloverhurst Avenue to Woodlawn Avenue, and the other runs southeast from Bobbin Mill Road to Westview Drive. The origin of this street name was not determined for sure, but few would doubt that it was named for Judge Hamilton McWhorter (1857-1929), who moved to Athens from Oglethorpe County in 1901 and bought Cloverhurst, the former home of Dr. Henry Hull Carlton (1834-1905) that he built in 1885.

Mealor Street was a one-block-long street that ran southwest from East Broad Street to Herring Street in East Athens. It no longer exists. The origin of this street name was not determined. The first reference found for this street was in the *Athens Daily Herald*, January 4, 1915.

Athens Streets & Neighborhoods

Meigs Street was named for Josiah Meigs (1757-1822), second president of the University of Georgia (1801-1810). Abraham Baldwin was the first president (1785-1801), but throughout his tenure, the university existed only on paper. Therefore, Meigs was the first president of UGA after the university was actually opened. See Bowdre Street.

Mell Street is a two-block-long street between Rutherford Street and Springdale Street, running parallel with Milledge Avenue. No doubt named for John Dagg Mell (1865-1952), a son of UGA Chancellor Patrick Hues Mell (1814-1888) and brother to Edward Baker Mell (1873-1959), beloved principal of Athens High School. John D. Mell was a lawyer, Baptist minister, UGA professor, president of the Board of Education, and solicitor of the city court. About 1910, John Mell bought the Lampkin/Charbonnier/Ashe house that was built on Jackson Street about 1840 and moved it to Milledge Avenue. Mell Street was created as the back boundary of Mell's property. The first reference found for this street was in the *Athens Banner*, September 8, 1911.

Miles Street is a one-block-long street that runs west off North Chase Street to Bryan Street. The origin of this street name was not determined. The first reference found for this street was in the *Athens Banner*, January 6, 1910.

Milledge Avenue begins at Prince Avenue and runs due south to Whitehall where it intersects with Whitehall Road and Simonton Bridge Road. Rowe (1923) wrote that this street was named for John Milledge (1757-1818), who bought and donated the land for the establishment of the University of Georgia and the city of Athens. Among his many accomplishments, Milledge served as governor of Georgia and U.S. senator from Georgia. Milledgeville, onetime capital of Georgia, was named for him.

Milledge Circle was cut in 1913 and terminates at the intersection of Lumpkin Street and Milledge Avenue to form Athens' famous Five Points.

Miller Street runs off Broad Street and is one block west of Rocksprings Street. It originally was two blocks long, one block north of Broad Street and one block south of Broad Street. The northern part of this street no longer exists. The origin of this street name was not determined. The first reference found for this street was in the *Weekly Banner-Watchman*, October 23, 1888.

Mitchell Bridge Road probably was named for William Letcher Mitchell who owned a large plantation in the area. There were two first cousins with this name in Athens. The older Mitchell (1798-1860) operated the Franklin House hotel for 25 years, early site of the Athens Post Office, where Mitchell was the postmaster. The younger William Letcher Mitchell (1805-1882) was a lawyer and was on the faculty of the University of Georgia. He was called "Slickhead" to distinguish him from his cousin. Mitchell Bridge Road probably was named for the younger cousin because he died in 1882 and the first reference found for Mitchell Bridge Road was in the *Banner Watchman*, September 23, 1884. For more information on the Mitchell cousins, see Charlotte Marshall's book, *Oconee Hill Cemetery of Athens, Georgia, Volume I*, pages 103, 286, and 287.

Mitchell Street was identified by the 1859 committee for naming streets as extending "from Prince Avenue toward Mitchell's

Mills." Mitchell's Mills was identified from a newspaper article in the *Athenian*, June 29, 1830, as belonging to Thomas Mitchell (1771-1852), who moved to Athens from Virginia and lived here for the last 48 years of his life. Therefore, Mitchell Street most likely was named for Thomas Mitchell. This Mitchell Street no longer exists and is not to be confused with the present Mitchell Street, formerly named Factory Street, that runs from Thomas Street to Williams Street.

Mitchell Street that now exists is one block long and extends from South Thomas Street to Williams Street. It formerly was named Factory Street. This street probably was named for William Letcher Mitchell who was the postmaster when the post office was located in his home near the top of Oconee Street hill, about one block from Mitchell Street. The first reference found for Mitchell Street was in the *Weekly Banner-Watchman*, December 11, 1888.

Morris Street was the former name of present-day Lyndon Avenue (also see). The namesake for Morris Street is not known for sure, but the most likely candidate is Casper Morris (1839-1890), an Athens businessman born in Filehne, Germany. He operated a large dry goods and millinery business on Broad Street for many years. He was unusual among Athens' Jewish community in that he joined the Confederate Army and fought for the South during the War Between the States. Casper Morris was a member of Co. D, 16th Georgia Volunteers, Cobb's Brigade. The first reference found for this street name was in the *Weekly Banner-Watchman*, October 2, 1888. Also see Morristown in the section on Athens Communities and Neighborhoods.

Morton Avenue (also seen as Morton Street) is described in the

Street Guide of the 1909 *Athens City Directory*, Morton Avenue as extending east from Fairview Avenue to White Street, one block north of Hampton Avenue. There were several prominent members of the Morton Family in Athens at this time, any of whom could have been honored by having this street named for them. However, perhaps the strongest candidate was John White Morton (1873-1936), a son of William J. Morton (1833-1918) and Rosena White Morton (1837-1933). John White Morton graduated from the University of Georgia and then spent a year studying in Europe. His youth was devoted to the family textile business as manager of Princeton Factory and the Star Thread Factory. In 1915 he became Cashier of the First National Bank of Athens, established by his grandfather John White in 1866. A short time later he became president of the bank, a position he held until his death. The first reference found for this street was as Morton Street in the *Athens Banner*, November 27, 1913.

Nacoochee Avenue is one of the new streets created when the Athens Park and Improvement Company developed a large tract of land north of Prince Avenue and west of Barber Street in the 1890s. (See Fig. 11). This is one of at least eight streets in the neighborhood that was given an Indian name. Nacoochee is the Anglicization of the Cherokee pronunciation of the Creek word, *Nokose*, which means "bear." The first reference found for Nacoochee Avenue was in the *Weekly Banner* on November 6, 1896.

Nantahala Avenue was another new street created when the Athens Park and Improvement Company developed a large tract of land north of Prince Avenue and west of Barber Street in the 1890s. (See Fig. 11). This is one of at least eight streets in the neighborhood given an Indian name. The word *Nantahala* is

Athens Streets & Neighborhoods

Cherokee and means Land of the Noonday Sun. The first reference found for Nantahala Avenue was in the *Athens Daily Banner* on May 5, 1893.

Narrow Street no longer exists. It was a narrow, one-block-long street between Lumpkin Street and Doboy Street, one block south of Baldwin Street and one block north of Sapelo Street. (See Fig. 9).

Nellie B Avenue was named for little 5-year-old Nell Pierce Brightwell (1889-1978), daughter of George Pierce Brightwell and Clara Talmage Brightwell. Nell was called Nellie as a child. Nell lived on the family farm on the Winterville Road until she was 17 years old. The family residence later became the home of AMVETS Post 10. The house no longer stands. Nellie's father was involved in creating a new street next to his property. Because Nellie was on the scene every day, the workmen jokingly referred to her as their "foreman" or "overseer," and her father decided to name the street for her. Nell Brightwell never married and died in 1978 at age 88. She is buried among family members in the Valley section of Oconee Hill Cemetery. The first reference found for Nellie B Avenue was in the *Weekly Banner*, July 5, 1895, and it also appears on Barnett's 1895 map of Athens.

Newton Street was most likely named for either John Hamlin Newton (1800-1889) or Elizur Lowrance Newton (1796-1882), two of Athens most prominent and respected citizens of their time. As far as can be determined, they were not related. The first references found for Newton Street was on W. W. Thomas' 1874 map of Athens and the name first appeared in the *Athens Weekly Georgian* November 7, 1876.

Gary L. Doster

Nichols Street was located in Oconee Heights and was named for Louis Harrison Nichols (1856-1918), a local merchant and farmer. At one time, the street was named School Street. It no longer exists. See Oconee Heights in the section on Athens Communities and Neighborhoods.

Nicholson Street was the former name of South View Drive until sometime in the 1940s. The street runs east and west between Milledge Avenue and East Campus Road. Nicholson Street probably was named for entrepreneur John William Nicholson (1824-1866), who first was in business with his brother-in-law William Sammons Grady (1821-1864) in the firm Grady & Nicholson. This partnership was dissolved in 1860 when Grady sold his share of the business to John William Nicholson, Edward Augustus Reaves, and Young H. Wynne. These three men continued the business under the name Nicholson, Reaves & Wynne. Circumstantial evidence that the street was named for John Nicholson is that he died April 30, 1886, and the first reference found for Nicholson Street was in the *Weekly Banner-Watchman* later that year on December 14, 1886.

Nisbet Street was identified by the 1859 street committee as extending "from Baldwin Street to Oconee [Hill] Cemetery." (See Fig. 15). According to Rowe in his 1923 *History of Athens & Clarke County, Georgia*, this street was named for Eugenius Aristides Nisbet (1803-1871). Nisbet was born near present-day Union Point in Greene County. He graduated from the University of Georgia in 1821 as the valedictorian of his class. He studied law under the tutelage of Augustin Smith Clayton in Athens. Nisbet served as a Georgia state representative from 1827 to 1829 and was a Georgia state senator from 1830 to 1835. In 1845, he became one of the first judges in the newly established Georgia Supreme Court, along with Joseph Henry Lumpkin and Hiram Warner. The name of Nisbet Street later was changed to Cemetery Street, then Jackson Street. Many years ago, the street was diverted slightly to the west to bypass the cemetery instead of leading directly into it and later became East Campus Drive.

North Avenue becomes Danielsville Road at the Athens city limits. Originally, North Avenue was known as River Street, Water Street, and Madison Avenue before it gained its present name.

Oakland Avenue—See **Habersham Street**.

Oconee Street was named for the Oconee River, which is an Indian name. This was the first street in Athens, and the first residences in Athens were built on this street as one travels up the hill from the river toward the intersection with Broad Street and Thomas Street.

O'Farrell Street probably was named for William Daniel O'Farrell (1851-1911), three-time mayor of Athens between 1883 and 1895. The first waterworks in Athens was built during his time as mayor, and sewerage service was extended from downtown into some residential areas. However, it is possible that the street was named for O'Farrell's brother James (1844-1901), who was the Athens Postmaster from 1893 to 1897. Furthermore, in his 1963 newspaper article, Jones Drewry credited William Daniel O'Farrell's son Ed with the honor because he was City Marshall for a number of years. The first reference found for this street was in the *Athens Banner*, October 10, 1913.

Olivia Street was in the same neighborhood as Helen Street and Marion Street. (See Fig. 7). All three streets ran off Carlton Avenue on the west side of South Milledge Avenue, directly behind Cloverhurst, the home of Dr. Henry Hull Carlton (1834-1905) and his wife, Helen Camak Newton Carlton (1844-1934). It is obvious that Helen Street, Marion Street, and Olivia Street were named for the daughters of H. H. and Helen Carlton; the three girls were the granddaughters of John Hamlin Newton (1800-1889) and Mary Jordan Newton (1904-1893). It is not certain that any of these streets existed other than on Barnett's 1895 Map of Athens, but Olivia Street may be the present site of Rutherford Street.

Oneida Street is also seen as Oneta Street and Onedia Street. This is one of the new streets created when the Athens Park and Improvement Company developed a large tract of land north of Prince Avenue and west of Barber Street in the 1890s. (See Fig. 11). The street forms the northern boundary of the development. It runs east and west and connects Chase Street and Barber Street. The origin of this street name was not determined, but it is one of at least eight streets in the neighborhood that were given an Indian name, so it could be for the Oneida Indians who originally occupied the area that later became central New York. The first reference seen in the local newspaper to the spelling Oneida was in the *Southern Watchman*, October 2, 1877. The first reference seen in the local newspaper to the spelling Oneta was in the *Athens Banner*, July 18, 1911. The first reference seen in the local newspaper to the spelling Onedia was in the *Athens Banner*, September 24, 1912. In the Street Guide on page 286 in the 1909 *Athens City Directory*, the street name is spelled Oneta.

Park Avenue is one of the main streets going from Prince Avenue to The Boulevard into the property developed in the 1890s as Athens Park and Improvement Company. (See Fig. 11).

Peabody Street no doubt was named for George Foster Peabody, one of the most generous benefactors of the University of Georgia in its history. Peabody was born in Columbus, Georgia, in 1852 and died at Warm Springs, Georgia, in 1938. The Peabody family originally came from Connecticut, and after the War Between the States, they moved to Brooklyn, New York. Peabody was a brilliant financier and became very wealthy. He retired in 1906 at the age of 54 and spent the rest of his life as one of the nation's most generous benefactors; especially favoring religious and educational charities. The first reference found for Peabody Street was in the *Athens Weekly Banner*, December 10, 1889.

Peter Street originally was named Peters Street, but this spelling was changed to Peter Street in modern times. (See Fig. 4). It is likely that the street was named for Richard Peters (1810-1889), a civil engineer from Germantown, Pennsylvania, who was involved with the construction of the Georgia Railroad from 1835 to 1845. As such, Peters would have been closely involved with bringing the railroad to Carr's Hill in Athens in 1840. Both Peter Street and Carr's Hill are located in East Athens. Richard Peters died in Atlanta in 1889, and the first reference found for Peters Street was in the *Athens Weekly Banner*, October 14, 1890; perhaps the street was named in his honor at that time.

Peters Street—See **Peter Street**.

Phinizy Street was identified by the 1859 committee for naming streets as running "from Oconee Street at Mr. Carr's toward Elberton to town limits." But later there also was another Phinizy Street in Athens. Neither exists by that name today. The first Phinizy Street is now referred to as Airport Road or Winterville Road. The other one originally was the west end of present-day Hancock Avenue, from Rocksprings Street to West Broad Street. (See Fig. 6). No doubt, both of these streets were named for Ferdinand Phinizy (1819-1889), the patriarch of the local Phinizy family. Phinizy was born in Oglethorpe County, Georgia, and came to Athens as a child in 1832. Phinizy married Harriet Hays Bowdre (1828-1863) and the couple had nine children before Harriet died. Phinizy then married Anne S. Barrett (1833-1924) and they had three children. Phinizy was immensly popular among Athenians, and it is thought that perhaps when Ferdinand Street was opened someone wanted to name it for him, but there already was a Phinizy Street, so they simply used his first name for this street. As further evidence of Phinizy's popularity, it also is thought that Bowdre Street, Jacob Street, Leonard Street, and Stewart Street were named for four of his sons. Having these streets named for Phinizy's children lends credibility to the theory that Ferdinand Street was named for Ferdinand Phinizy. That neighborhood has been drastically altered over the years, and none of these streets exist by these names today.

Plantation Road appears on W. W. Thomas' 1874 Map of Athens as the northern end of Milledge Avenue Extension that branched off from Milledge Avenue at the present-day intersection of Gran Ellen Drive and Pinecrest Court and now ends at the Athens Bypass. It is not known whose plantation Thomas was referring to. (See Fig. 2).

Plum Nelly Road is located between Westview Drive on the south and Rocky Ford Road on the north, just off West Lake Drive. As the road runs north, it forms a circle and joins back with itself just before it terminates at Rocky Ford Road. When I was a child growing up in Athens, I remember hearing that this street was so named because it was "plum out of town and 'nelly' out of the county." I have no idea as to the veracity of this story, but I have always believed it.

Pope Street was said by Rowe (1923) to be named for Gen. Burwell Pope, Jr. (1790-1840), who commanded the Georgia Brigade during the War of 1812. Pope was married to Sarah Key Strong, who outlived him by 37 years. When Gen. Pope died in 1840, he was interred in the old Athens Cemetery on Jackson Street, alongside his son Charles, who died in 1839 at age 17 while a student at the University of Georgia. By the time Sarah died in 1877, Oconee Hill Cemetery was open, and she owned a lot there, which is where she was buried. In her will she provided for her late husband and son to be exhumed and buried in her lot in Oconee Hill Cemetery. Pope Street extends north from Baxter Street, across Broad Street, and across Prince Avenue. The first reference found for this street name was in the *Southern Banner*, January 5, 1860.

Pottery Street originally was a three-block-long, dead-end street located one block south of East Broad Street, running east and west across Willow Street and Wilkerson Street. (See Fig. 16). The street extended to the tracks of the Georgia Railroad on the western end and to the North Oconee River on the eastern end. In modern times the eastern and western ends of Pottery Street were abolished, and the street presently runs west from

Wilkerson Street for one block, then turns due north for one block and dead ends into East Broad Street. This street was so named because of the establishment of the Athens Pottery here in 1884. The business was started by Robert Lee Bloomfield, and Cameron Douglas Flanigen (1854-1942) was his general manager. The business was founded to manufacture clay sewer pipe, flower pots, and jugs. Apparently, the business failed and was closed in the early 1890s. However, in 1911 the factory was reopened under new management. The new owners were brothers W. A. Harsha and T. R. Harsha from East Liverpool, Ohio, with F. B. Hinton as president and George Williams as secretary-treasurer. Twenty-five skilled pottery workers and their families were moved to Athens from the north to produce a wide variety of pots, jugs, jars, and vases. The business flourished for a while, but eventually it too failed and went out of business. The property and assets of the company were sold by the bankruptcy court February 18, 1916.

Pound Street is a three-block-long street that begins across Prince Avenue from the old State Normal School campus and runs northeast from Prince Avenue to Nantahala Avenue Extension. Undoubtedly, this street was named for Jere Madison Pound (1864-1935), born in Liberty Hill, Georgia, educated at the University of Georgia, and was one of the most prolific educators of his time. Pound served as principal of Fort Valley [Georgia] Institute; president of Gordon Institute in Barnesville, Georgia; director of the Department of Education of the Georgia Normal and Industrial College at Milledgeville (later named Georgia State College for Women, now named the Georgia College & State University); superintendent of the East Florida Seminary in Gainesville, Florida; Superintendent of Georgia State Schools; and from 1912 to 1933,

Pound was president of the State Normal School and Teachers College in Athens. Pound Auditorium on the Normal School campus also is named for him. Pound's final position was as president of the Georgia State Women's College at Valdosta, Georgia, where he served for one year before poor health forced him to take a leave of absence. He died a few months later in Athens and was buried in Barnesville, Georgia.

Prince Avenue originally was called Federal Road. When Athens was established, it was the main road going north into Indian country. That name Federal Road was maintained until after the death of Oliver Hillhouse Prince (1782-1837), who retired in 1836, moved to Athens, and bought a large farm on that road just at the then Athens city limits. Prince's property was in the vicinity of present-day University of Georgia Medical College, formerly the U.S. Navy Supply Corps School; prior to that, the property was the campus of University Demonstration School, and prior to that it was the State Normal School. After only sixteen months in Athens, Prince and his wife were lost at sea when sailing from Boston to Charleston, and the steamship they were on was wrecked in a storm. Sometime after the deaths of Mr. and Mrs. Prince, the Federal Road was renamed in their honor. The first reference found for the name Prince Avenue was in the *Southern Banner*, April 7, 1859.

Prince Place is a one-block-long street between Prince Avenue and Cobb Street that formerly was the 600 block of Chase Street. It has not been determined exactly when the name of this block was changed from Chase Street to Prince Place, but the first reference found for that name was in the *Athens Banner*, July 21, 1917. Various stories have circulated about why this happened, one being that a new resident on this block did not want a Chase Street address because its western end extended into a poorer neighborhood, and the person had enough influence with the City Fathers to be successful in having the name changed. At least three individuals have been named as the one responsible but it is not known for sure who it was.

Princeton Road or **Princeton Factory Road** was an early name for South Lumpkin Street, which also was sometimes referred to as Watkinsville Road. (See Fig. 2).

Public Street— See **Broad Street**.

Pulaski Heights is a one-block-long street that runs west off Pulaski Street to Hendricks Avenue. In modern times, the residents along Pulaski Heights and the northern part of Pulaski Street have unofficially named their entire neighborhood Pulaski Heights, and the designation has been generally accepted by the public. Also see Pulaski Street.

Pulaski Street runs north and south between Broad Street and Cleveland Avenue. The origin of the name is the same as Pulaski Heights. The street was named for Count Casimir Pulaski, a Polish general who assisted the American colonists during the American Revolution. Pulaski was killed in 1779 while defending Savannah against the British. Numerous counties, towns, streets, and other edifices have been named for Pulaski throughout the eastern United States. The first reference found for Pulaski Street was in the *Southern Watchman*. April 14, 1857.

Reese Street probably was named for Dr. Charles Milton Reese

(1788-1862), according to Rowe (1923). Rowe avowed that he was the most prominent person named Reese who ever lived in Athens. Reese was a physician who previously served as a surgeon in the Italian army for eight years. The first reference found for this street was in the *Southern Banner*, June 9, 1859, when the eastern part of School Street was renamed Reese Street. At the same time, the western part of School Street was named Taylor Street, but eventually this also became Reese Street.

Rhodes Street is located in Oconee Heights and was named for Alexander Stephens Rhodes (1861-1923), an Athens entrepreneur. The street apparently still exists as part of Ambler Road. See Oconee Heights in the section on Athens Communities and Neighborhoods for more information.

River Street was an early name for Water Street/Madison Avenue/North Avenue. The 1859 street committee said this street went "from Thomas Street at Mr. Barry's over the Upper Bridge and on toward Danielsville to town limits."

Rocksprings Street was named for the large spring that emanated from near the present-day intersection of Hill Street and The Plaza. The spring and much of its stream were covered over many years ago and piped underground to the Middle Oconee River.

Roseland Street was changed to Stanton Way in 1932 to honor Lucy May Stanton (1875-1931). The origin of the name of Roseland Street is not known. See Stanton Way for information on Lucy May Stanton.

Russell Avenue ran northwest off Barrett Street (now Ruth Street), parallel with Hughes Avenue. The origin of this street name is not known for certain, but it very well could have been named for Judge William John Russell (1825-1897) or his son Richard Brevard Russell, Sr. (1861-1938), chief justice of the Georgia Supreme Court, or his grandson R. B. Russell, Jr. (1897-1971), governor of Georgia (1931-1933) and U.S. senator from Georgia (1933-1971). Judge Russell owned Timothy Heights farm near the Princeton Community off Highway 441/15. Russell Avenue and Hughes Avenue no longer exist. Also see Timothy Road.

Ruth Street formerly was named Barrett Street and Water Street. This street begins when present-day Elizabeth Street crosses to the east side of the North Oconee River. Ruth Street continues northward to connect with River Street/Water Street/Madison Avenue/North Avenue. The origin of the name for Ruth Street is not known. See Phinizy Street for the possible source of the name for Barrett Street.

Rutherford Street probably was named for Williams Rutherford (1818-1896), an 1838 graduate of the University of Georgia and long-time honored professor at the university. Rutherford married Laura Battaile Cobb (1818-1888), sister of Howell Cobb, Sr. and Thomas R. R. Cobb. The first reference found for Rutherford Street was in the *Weekly Banner*, February 10, 1899.

Sanford Drive undoubtedly was named for Dr. Steadman Vincent Sanford (1871-1945), president of the University of Georgia (1932-1935) and promoter of athletics at UGA. The football stadium also is named for Dr. Sanford. The street extends east from Baldwin Street between Sanford Stadium and Tate Student Center, across Cedar Street, to Carlton Street.

Sapelo Street no longer exists. It ran east from Lumpkin Street for one block and dead ended into Doboy Street at the approximate location of present-day Tate Student Center. (See Fig. 9). Some of Athens' most prominent early families had strong ties to Sapelo Island, Georgia, and visited there often. Sapelo Sound borders the northern tip of Sapelo Island, and Doboy Sound is on the southern end. No doubt Sapelo Street was named for Sapelo Sound because of the affection these Athenians had for the area. The first reference found for Sapelo Street was in the *Banner-Watchman*, May 19, 1889. Also see Doboy Street.

Satula Avenue (first spelled Satulah) was one of the new streets created when the Athens Park and Improvement Company developed a large tract of land north of Prince Avenue and west of Barber Street in the 1890s. (See Fig. 11). The first reference found for the spelling Satulah was in the *Weekly* Banner on September 4, 1908. The first reference found for the spelling Satula was in the *Athens Banner* on February 25, 1910. The names were used interchangeably through the early 1920s. The origin of this name was not determined for certain, but it probably was named for Satulah Mountain in North Carolina. It is assumed to be an Indian name. This is likely, because there are at least seven other streets in the neighborhood that were given Indian names: Chatooga, Hiawassee, Nacoochee, Nantahala, Oneta, Seminole, and Yonah.

School Street was the street immediately south of Lucy Cobb Institute, running east and west from Rocksprings Street to Pulaski Street. According to an Athens newspaper dated June 9, 1859, the eastern end of School Street was renamed Reese Street, and the western end was renamed Taylor Street, but Taylor Street also eventually was changed to Reese Street.

School Street also was the name of a street in the community of Oconee Heights on the north side of town. At one time this street was named Church Street. For more information, see Oconee Heights in the section on Athens Communities and Neighborhoods.

Scott Street originally ran south from South Lumpkin Street to Hampton Avenue (now Hampton Court); now it is a three-block-long street that runs south from Morton Avenue to South View Drive. The origin of this street name was not determined. The first reference found for Scott Street was in the *Athens Banner*, December 13, 1895.

Seminole Avenue was one of the new streets created when the Athens Park and Improvement Company developed a large tract of land north of Prince Avenue and west of Barber Street in the 1890s. (See Fig. 11). This is one of at least eight streets in the neighborhood that was given an Indian name. The word *Seminole* is a corruption of *cimarrón*, a Spanish term for runaway or wild one. The first reference found for Seminole Avenue was in the *Weekly Banner* on May 12, 1899.

Simons Street is a one-block-long street that connects East Broad Street and Branch Street in East Athens. The origin of this street name was not determined.

Smith Street is a two-block-long street that runs south off South Lumpkin Street, parallel with Carlton Street. Two individuals who may have had this street named for them were Edward Inglis Smith, Sr. (1854-1828), two-term Athens mayor from 1898 to 1901, or Paul Lloyd Smith, who became postmaster of Athens in 1922.

Athens Streets & Neighborhoods

Soule Street is a one-block-long street that runs north and south connecting D. W. Brooks Drive and Sanford Drive on the University of Georgia campus. No doubt named for Andrew McNairn Soule (1872-1934), who came to the University of Georgia in 1907 as president of the newly created College of Agricultural and Mechanical Arts. At the same time, he also was appointed as dean of the College of Agriculture. Soule maintained those positions until shortly before his death in 1933. Because of his aggressive efforts regarding coeducation, the first women's dormitory on the UGA campus also was named for him.

Spring Street is one block south of Broad Street and originally led to the town spring, from which early Athenians obtained their drinking water.

Standard Oil Street (also seen as Standard Oil Road) is an unpaved, one-block-long, dead-end street that runs south off Cleveland Avenue parallel with the railroad tracks. This street used to lead to a Standard Oil Company warehouse and storage tanks for oil and gasoline, which are now gone. The first reference found for this street was in the *Athens Daily Herald*, January 1, 1914.

Stanton Way formerly was named Roseland Street. The name was changed to Stanton Way in 1932 to honor Lucy May Stanton (1875-1931), world-famous artist. This is one of the few Athens streets known to be named for a woman. Miss Stanton painted landscapes, portraits, and still lifes, but she was particularly well-known for her miniature portrait paintings. Miss Stanton was born in Atlanta, Georgia, and graduated with honors from Southern Female College (now Cox College) in LaGrange, Georgia, in 1893. She lived, worked, studied, taught, and exhibited all over the

United States and Europe, and some of her works remain in the collections of the National Portrait Gallery in Washington, D.C., the Metropolitan Museum of Art in New York, the Museum of Fine Arts in Boston, the Philadelphia Museum of Art, and in other prestigious collections. In Atlanta, she lived across the street from Joel Chandler Harris and painted a famous, award-winning watercolor portrait on ivory of Harris in 1914 after his death. The portrait of Harris is in the collection of the National Portrait Gallery of the Smithsonian Institution. Among her other famous works is a portrait of Howell Cobb, Sr., who was Speaker of the U.S. House of Representatives, and that painting is in the collection of the House of Representatives. Miss Stanton's sister, Willie Marion Stanton, was married to Athenian Walter T. Forbes. In 1908 or 1909, Lucy Stanton built an art studio in the Cobbham community of Athens, and she lived in Athens intermittently when not traveling. In 1926, she moved to Athens permanently and lived here the rest of her life. Miss Stanton was one of the founders of the Athens Y.W.C.A. in 1910 and the Athens Women's Suffrage League in 1912. Lucy May Stanton died March 19, 1931, and is buried in Oconee Hill Cemetery.

States' Rights Street — see **Henderson Avenue**.

Stegeman Drive was a short dead-end street that ran east from South Lumpkin Street to the eventual site of Stegeman Hall, toward the present site of Sanford Stadium. This street no longer exists. Stegeman Drive no doubt was named for Herman James Stegeman (1891-1939), famous athletic coach at the University of Georgia from 1919 to 1938. An accomplished athlete in several sports himself, at UGA Stegeman variously coached baseball, basketball, football, and track and field. He also served as Dean of Men at UGA from 1931 to 1938. In addition to the now-demolished Stegeman Hall, Stegeman Coliseum also was named for Coach Stegeman.

Stevens Street actually is Stephens Street, but the name apparently was misspelled when it was listed in the 1920-21 *Athens City Directory*. There also was a reference to Stevens Street in the *Weekly Banner*, August 9, 1918. See Stephens Street.

Stephens Street ran north from Atlanta Avenue, one block east of Barber Street, according to the Street Guide in the 1909 *Athens City Directory*. The street no longer exists. The origin of this street name was not determined, but it would not be unreasonable to think that it was named for Alexander Hamilton Stephens, Vice-President of the Confederate States of America. Stephens was a graduate of the University of Georgia and lived in nearby Crawfordville, Georgia.

Stewart Street is shown on Barnett's 1895 map of Athens as a one-block-long street that connected "old" Clover Street (present-day Hillcrest Avenue) with the southwest end of Phinizy Street (present-day Hancock Avenue). (See Fig. 6). This street apparently never existed except "on paper," and it is thought that it was one of several Athens streets that were named for members of the Phinizy Family. Also see Barrett, Bowdre, Jacob, Leonard, Phinizy and Stewart streets.

Stonewall Avenue ran west from Madison Avenue/North Avenue across Barrett Street (now Ruth Street), parallel with Long Avenue and Woods Avenue. Stonewall Avenue, Long Avenue, and Woods Avenue no longer exist. Although it has not been documented, surely this street was named for Confederate General Thomas Jonathan "Stonewall" Jackson (1824-1863), southern hero of the War Between the States.

Strickland Street is a short street connecting Dr. Martin Luther King, Jr. Parkway and North Avenue. The origin of this street name was not determined. The first reference found for this street name was in the *Athens Daily Banner*, December 10, 1897.

Strong Street originally was six blocks long and extended from Hull Street on the western end to Willow Street on the east. One block on the western end and two blocks on the eastern end were lost to modern development, and Strong Street now is only three blocks long. Rowe (1923) identified this street as being named for Elisha Strong (1792-1879), an Athens merchant. Strong was the son of Charles Strong (1764-1848), a Revolutionary War soldier who brought his family from Virginia to Oglethorpe County, Georgia, in 1800. Charles Strong and his wife, Sarah Key Strong, died in Oglethorpe County and were buried in Arnoldsville but were moved to Oconee Hill Cemetery in Athens in the mid-1920s. Charles' son Elisha moved to Athens and was a prosperous merchant in the 1830s and early 1840s. He lived in the block where College Avenue School was eventually built, now bounded by College Avenue, Jackson Street, Madison Avenue, and Strong Street. This is the current site of Hotel Indigo. The house was not demolished but was moved to the corner of Milledge Avenue and Rutherford Street by the Mell family. The house eventually was demolished in the 1960s and was replaced by the Zeta Tau Alpha sorority house. Elisha Strong moved his family to Monroe County, Mississippi, in the early 1840s, where he became a successful planter. Elisha had married Ann Scott Hill (c.1804-1878) in Oglethorpe County on September 18, 1821. After 56 years of marriage, Ann died February 8, 1878, and, like many older married couples, Elisha did not live long after Ann's death and died nine months later in November 1878. Elisha and Ann are buried in the Odd Fellows Rest Cemetery in Aberdeen, Mississippi. Elisha joined Alexander's Battalion of Riflemen during the War of 1812, and by the time he was discharged he had been promoted to 2nd lieutenant. However, as was common with successful businessmen of his day, later as a mature adult he acquired the title of colonel. Furthermore, according to his 1878 obituary, by the time of his death he had been promoted to general!

Summey Street was a one-block-long, dead-end street that ran east from South Lumpkin Street just south of Sapelo Street. (See Fig. 9). The street no longer exists. Summey is not a common name in the Athens area, and this street no doubt was named for Peter A. Summey (1811-1891), who came to Athens from North Carolina in 1843 and became a successful merchant in the firm Summey & Newton. Summey also was one of the organizers of the Athens Steam Company in 1850 and the Bank of Athens in 1858. During the War Between the States, Summey was a member of the famed Mitchell Thunderbolts, a homeguard unit comprised of older Athens men.

Tabernacle Street originally was a one-block-long street that ran northeast from Oak Street to Branch Street. The street eventually was extended across Branch Street to connect with Dublin Street, which began at East Broad Street. The name of Tabernacle Street was changed to Dublin Street. The first reference found for Tabernacle Street was in the 1889 *Athens City Directory* when the East

Athens Methodist Church was located there. The pastor was Rev. H. M. Quillian, and the Sunday School Supertintendant was A. H. Saye.

Tallulah Avenue (also called **Tallulah Street**) intersected with Chatuga Avenue, and it is speculated that both names were derived from Rabun County in Northeast Georgia, Tallulah Falls and the Chatuga (also Chatooga) River. According to an article in the January 4, 1923, *Athens Daily Herald* (p.1), the name of Tallulah Avenue was changed to West View Drive on January 3, 1923. Later, the name of Chatuga Avenue was changed to Woodland Way. The first reference found for Tallulah Street was in the *Athens Daily Herald*, January 1, 1914. The first reference found for Chatooga Avenue was in the *Athens Banner*, June 28, 1912.

Talmadge Drive and **Talmadge Street** likely were named for Clovis Gerdine Talmadge (1845-1896), three-term mayor of Athens in 1876, 1877, and 1880. However, there were several prominent members of the Talmadge Family living in Athens, and either or both of these streets could have been named for the entire family. In 1869, Clovis Talmadge and his younger brother John established Talmadge Brothers, a wholesale grocery business. Later, they partnered with the Hodgson Brothers to form Talmadge, Hodgson & Company. When this partnership was disbanded, Clovis and John reorganized the business as Talmadge Brothers & Company. After Clovis died, John brought his four sons into the business and it continued for many years as Talmadge Brothers & Company, Wholesale Groceries. The first reference found for Talmadge Street was in the *Athens Daily Herald*, October 28, 1913. The first reference found for Talmadge Drive was in the 1949 *Athens City Directory*.

Taylor Street probably was named for General Robert Taylor (1787-1859). General Taylor built the house known today as the Taylor-Grady House on Prince Avenue in about 1845. In 1853, he gave the house to his son Richard Deloney Bolling Taylor (1830-1864) as a wedding gift when he married Sarah Jane Billups. The first reference found for this street was in the *Southern Banner*, June 9, 1859, the year General Taylor died, when the western part of School Street was renamed Taylor Street. The name of Taylor Street eventually was changed to Reese Street.

Thomas Street was originally known as "Alley No. 2" in the early history of Athens, according to Hull's *Annals of Athens, Georgia* (pg. 4). The street was named for Stevens Thomas (1814-1891), the principle Athens merchant of his time. Thomas had his store on Broad Street at the corner with Thomas Street. This corner now is occupied by Main Street Bank (475 East Broad Street). Stevens Thomas' home was behind the store and faced Thomas Street.

Tibbetts Avenue is a one-block-long street that runs east and west to connect Nacoochee Avenue and Hiawassee Avenue, just north of Boulevard. The street probably was named for John Francis Tibbetts (1868-1958), a native of Sanford, Maine, who was the manager of the old Southern Mill across the railroad tracks from the Athens Park and Improvement Company community. Tibbetts also was involved with the operation of Athens Railway & Electric Company.

Tibbetts Street is a one-block-long street that runs west off Pulaski Street and connects with Hendricks Avenue. Tibbetts Street originally was established as Gantt Street in November 1884. The name was changed to Tibbetts Street on February 6, 1908. The origin of the street name is the same as Tibbetts Avenue.

Tilden Street was named for Samuel Jones Tilden (1814-1886), Democratic candidate for U.S. President in 1876. Tilden actually won the election according to the popular vote, but the office was awarded to Rutherford B. Hayes by the Electoral College because of a supposed discrepancy in the vote count. The location of this street could not be determined, and it is possible that it existed only on paper. Also see Cleveland Avenue.

Timothy Road led to Timothy Heights, a farm owned by Judge William John Russell (1825-1897), father of Richard Brevard Russell, Sr. (1861-1938), Chief Justice of the Georgia Supreme Court. Judge Russell's grandson, R. B. Russell, Jr. (1897-1971), was governor of Georgia and U.S. senator from Georgia. Timothy Heights was in the Princeton Community off Highway 441/15. The name of the farm probably was derived from Timothy grass, which is used to make high-quality Timothy hay. In addition to R. B. Russell Sr. and Jr., there were several other prominent members of the Russell Family, including Lewis C. Russell (1871-1950), another son of William John Russell, owner of Timothy Heights farm. Lewis Russell's obituary in the March 8, 1950, edition of the *Banner-Herald* indicated that he was born in the "...old Russell home at Princeton, where the Russell family lived for 22 years."

Trilby Street is a one-block-long street that connects Oconee

Street and Georgia Drive (formerly Georgia Depot Street). The origin of this street name was not determined.

Upson's Alley is a one-block-long, dead-end street that extends west from Nacoochee Avenue one block North of Prince Avenue. The most prominent member of the Upson Family in Athens was Judge Stephen Cummins Upson (1823-1914), and it is likely that this street was named for him. Upson was born in Lexington, Georgia, graduated with a law degree from Yale in 1841, then attended school in Paris before returning to Lexington to practice law. He moved to New York and practiced law for several years before moving back to Lexington. He came to Athens in 1885 and bought the Marcus A. Franklin house on Prince Avenue built in 1846. Upson remodeled the house and lived there the rest of his life. This house was home to the Trust Company Bank of Northeast Georgia for many years, but they relocated in 2017.

Waddell Street was named for Moses Waddel (1770-1840), fifth president of the University of Georgia (1819-1829). His son James Pleasants Waddel (1801-1867) was professor of ancient languages at UGA, and his grandson William Henry Waddel (1834-1878) taught languages and literature at UGA. Moses spelled his name Waddel and pronounced it to rhyme with bottle. Some of his descendants adopted the spelling as Waddell and put the accent on the second syllable; which is the way the street name is spelled.

Wall Street is a one-block-long street between Thomas Street and Jackson Street that connects Broad Street with Clayton Street. (See Fig. 14). It was one of the earliest named streets in Athens, and the first reference found for Wall Street was in the *Southern Whig*, December 29, 1838. The origin of this street name has not been determined, and it is not known if the street was named for a person or a thing. However, an exhaustive search of many references on Athens and Georgia did not disclose anyone named Wall who was prominent in our early history.

Walton Street—See **Dougherty Street**.

Wanassed Street was a one-block-long, dead-end street that ran east off of South Billups Street two blocks south of West Broad Street and one block east of Rocksprings Street. According to Milton Leathers, when this street was new and unnamed, someone scribbled "Unassigned" on the map, and it was mistakenly deciphered as Wanassed. The street was obliterated in 2016 and its former site is the border of a large parking lot on the north end of Clarke Central High School.

Ware Street probably was named for Dr. Edward Roswell Ware, who was elected as the first Intendant (Mayor) of Athens in 1848 and served four successive terms. Prior to Ware's election, the title for this office had been chairman. This street originally ran east from North Lumpkin Street, crossed College Avenue, and went to the North Oconee River. It currently is a one-block-long, dead-end street that goes west from North Lumpkin Street. The first reference found for Ware Street was in the *Weekly Banner-Watchman*, July 20, 1886.

Warren Street extends north from Vine Street to Fairview Street in East Athens. The origin of this street name has not been determined.

Washington Street most likely was named for President George

Washington, as were scores of streets in other American towns across the country. Early in the history of Athens, this was the original name of the street. When the Town Hall and Market House was built in the middle of Washington Street between Lumpkin and Hull streets in 1845, the name was unofficially changed to Market Street and it existed under that name for many years (See Fig. 13). When the county seat of Clarke County was moved from Watkinsville to Athens in 1872, the Town Hall became the Clarke County Courthouse. After a new courthouse was completed on Prince Avenue in 1876, the old Town Hall/Market House/Courthouse was sold and relocated from the middle of the street to the north side of the street and rebuilt as a livery stable. A few years later, the building was remodeled as Athens Carriage and Wagon Works. On October 10, 1893, the building was destroyed by fire. In 1912, the name of Market Street was changed back to Washington Street.

Water Street was identified in the 1859 street committee's list as running "From Lower Bridge on the river to Baldwin street." This would mean that this street was on the west side of the North Oconee River and was the name of present-day Williams Street. However, the Water Street known to modern Athenians was on the east side of the river and extended from the Cook and Brother Armory (later Chicopee Mill) to Madison Avenue/North Avenue and at one time went as far as to include present-day Ruth Street. Water Street became Armory Road after the Cook brothers built their armory there during the War Between the States. This street now is named Dr. Martin Luther King, Jr. Parkway. Also see Hobson Avenue.

Watkinsville Road was an early name for both Lumpkin Street and Milledge Avenue. (See Fig. 2).

West View Drive—see **Tallulah Street**.

White Avenue was named for John White (1799-1881), who was born in Ireland and came to Athens in 1837 to operate Georgia Factory at Whitehall, which he eventually bought. White became a prosperous businessman and was a founder of the National Bank of Athens.

White Street originally was named Gilmer Street. This was a one-block-long street that ran east and west to connect South Hull Street with South Lumpkin Street. The street was abolished in modern times to allow for the expansion of the Holiday Inn. White street probably was named for John White, who is identified under White Avenue above and also under Whitehall in the section on Athens Communities and Neighborhoods.

Wilcox Street is a one-block-long street that connects East Rutherford Street to Bloomfield Street. The origin of the name of this street has not been determined. The first reference found for Wilcox Street was in the *Athens Daily Herald*, May 30, 1922.

Wilkerson Street is a two-block-long street connecting Oconee Street with Broad Street near the North Oconee River. (See Fig. 16). The street no doubt was named for Col. Isaac Wilkerson (1801-1877) who lived in the area. In his *Annals of Athens, Georgia*, A. L. Hull identified Wilkerson's house as a "chateau" built by Madame Gouvain between Foundry Street and the North Oconee River. Hull further stated that Madame Gouvain's chateau later became home to Catherine Lowrance Newton (1756-1846) and her children when they moved here from Oglethorpe County after the death of her husband, Rev. John Newton. Later, this house was enlarged and became the "Wilkerson Place." The Wilkerson house eventually was removed to make room for the Georgia Railroad Depot that occupied the site for more than one hundred years. Isaac Wilkerson may have lived in another house near or on Wilkerson Street before acquiring the Gouvain-Newton house. The first reference found for Wilkerson Street was in the November 13, 1888, *Weekly Banner-Watchman*.

Williams Street was described by the 1859 committee on naming streets which stated that Williams Street went "From Thomas street back of old Female school to College Avenue." The current Williams Street runs from the foot of Oconee Street hill westward for two blocks and ends where Baldwin Street begins. The origin of this street name was not determined, but a likely candidate is William Williams (1786-1845) who moved to Athens from Hancock County in 1817. Williams was one of the founders and directors of the Georgia Rail Road in the 1830s and 1840s, and by 1836 he had acquired all of the stock in Princeton Factory and became the sole owner.

Woodland Way—see **Chatuga Avenue**.

Woodlawn Avenue—See **Adams Street**.

Woods Avenue ran west from Madison Avenue/North Avenue across Barrett Street (now Ruth Street), in the neighborhood of the family of Joseph White Woods (1839-1922) and Emma Conger Woods (1852-1935), and undoubtedly was named for that family or some individual member of the family. Three of John and Emma's daughters were prominent teachers in the Athens schools for many years: Elizabeth Groves Woods (1885-1954), Emma Ellice Woods (1887-1952), and Mary Etta Woods (1888-1987).

Wray Street most likely was named for Thomas Wray (1805-1860), successful planter who lived on Wray Street and built the Wray-Nicholson House on Hull Street in 1848-1849.

Wynburn Avenue (also called Wynburn Place; also spelled Wynbourne Avenue) is a two-block-long street that runs from Boulevard to Chatooga. It was one of the new streets created when the Athens Park and Improvement Company developed a large tract of land north of Prince Avenue and west of Barber Street in the 1890s. (See Fig. 11). The origin of this street name was not determined. The first reference found for Wynburn Avenue was in the December 11, 1896, issue of the *Weekly Banner*. The first reference found for Wynburn Place was in the July 19, 1905, *Athens Banner*.

Yonah Avenue formerly was named Buena Vista Avenue. It was one of the new streets created when the Athens Park and Improvement Company developed a large tract of land north of Prince Avenue and west of Barber Street in the 1890s. (See Fig. 11). This is one of at least eight streets in the neighborhood that was given an Indian name. In Cherokee, Yonah means "*bear*." The first reference found for Yonah Avenue was in the *Weekly Banner* on December 18, 1896.

Some Athens Communities and Neighborhoods

Allenville was an African-American neighborhood located a few blocks south of present-day Five Points, between South Milledge Avenue and Milledge Avenue Extension near the present-day intersection of Gran Ellen Drive and Pinecrest Court. The settlement is shown quite prominently on W. W. Thomas' 1874 map of Athens as Alenville [sic]. (See Fig. 2). That part of Milledge Avenue was called Georgia Factory Road, and Milledge Avenue Extension was called Plantation Road, although the space between the two streets is considerably different today.

According to Steven Brown's research (personal communication):...in 1874 the Georgia Factory or Whitehall Road strikes off from Five Points (then four points) up Milledge Terrace and, as shown on the 1874 map, makes a sharp turn onto the current route of Carlton Terrace, running roughly parallel to Church's "Homeplace"—at that time owned by F.W. Lucas. It continues along the gentler Carlton Terrace slope as long as it can until it descends to join the route of Milledge Extension, the original roadbed at the Gran Ellen point. Looking at drainage, this steers it well around the ravine that opens just south of Hampton Court and just east of Milledge, eventually flowing down into Lake Herrick, as well as the ravines south of Gran Ellen.

The Allenville community flourished in the late 1800s and early 1900s and had the reputation of being the home of some of Athens' most prominent African-American families. An African-American school was located in Allenville in one room of a neighborhood African-American church (Thankful Baptist Church?). All that remains of Allenville today is the large Charity of Love Cemetery that obviously was associated with the church. The triangular-shaped cemetery is just over an acre in size and fronts on South Milledge Avenue, with 1728 South Milledge Avenue on the south side, and on the northwest it borders on the back boundaries of five residential lots on Annes Court. According to *Athens-Clarke County, Georgia Cemeteries* (1999) edited by Eve B. Weeks for the Athens Historical Society, in addition to about 20 graves with readable headstones, "There are at least 37 marked graves with no inscription or unreadable inscriptions...and at least 30 unmarked graves visible, probably many more that were not seen due to the ivy covering the ground." There are a few graves located across the street on the other side of Milledge Avenue.

Athens Park and Improvement Company was established by a group of Athens businessmen in 1890 (See Fig. 11). The group bought 300 acres of undeveloped land bordered by Prince Avenue on the south, Barber Street on the east, and the Georgia, Carolina, and Northern Railroad on the north. This project was undertaken after an agreement was made with the Athens Street Railway Company to replace their little mule-drawn streetcars with electric cars and extend their tracks from downtown Athens to this area. Several new Athens streets were created when this large unimproved tract of land was developed. The main thoroughfare going east and west through the development is The Boulevard. For an excellent commentary on this neighborhood and a superb map of the area, see page 77 in James K. Reap's book, *Athens, A Pictorial History* (The Donning Company, Norfork, VA, 1992).

Athens Water Works was located on a section of Tanyard Branch on the west side of South Lumpkin Street until it was moved to a location on the North Oconee River in the early 1890s. (See Fig. 9 and 10). Legion Pool was opened at the old water works site on June 7, 1936.

Barberville Community was sited around the northern end of present-day North Avenue and formerly was dominated by the Barber, Conger, and Woods families. The community was named for "Wed" Barber. See Barber Street in the section on street names.

Blairsville Community was a white neighborhood located at the intersection of South Lumpkin Street and South Milledge Avenue—the community now called Five Points (See Fig. 2). Blairsville was an unpaved rural crossroads where Lumpkin Street and Milledge Avenue met before Milledge Circle joined the intersection in 1913 to form Five Points. Blairsville was near the city limits of Athens at that time, and as the community grew it expanded down South Lumpkin Street toward the Princeton Community instead of down South Milledge Avenue toward the African-American community of Allenville. In the early days, South Lumpkin Street was alternately identified as Princeton Road, Princeton Factory Road, and Watkinsville Road. At the same time, South Milledge Avenue was known as Georgia Factory Road because it led to Whitehall, the location of John White's Georgia Factory. Milledge Avenue also was sometimes called Simonton

Bridge Road or Watkinsville Road because when one arrived in Whitehall, a right turn would place you on the Simonton Bridge Road, which led to Watkinsville.

Circumstantial evidence strongly suggests that Blairsville was named for an early resident, William D. Blair (1831-1884), who bought a total of three and five-eighths acres of land in the South fork of South Lumpkin Street and South Milledge Avenue in 1871, 1873, 1875, and 1878 (Clarke County Deed Book Z, page 474; Deed Book BB, page 270; Deed Book BB, page 271; and Deed Book BB, page 272). One of the first references to Blairsville was in the obituary of William D. Blair in the *Banner Watchman* on July 22, 1884. According to census records, William D. Blair was a cabinet maker born in Clarke County on June 6, 1831. He married Martha J. Pridgeon (1837-1888) on November 22, 1857. The Blair's oldest child was Merritt Ophelia Blair (1859-1930), who married General Daniel Parr (1855-1916) in 1878 (General was Parr's given name and not a military title). When G. D. Parr and Ophelia Blair were married, W. D. Blair sold three quarters of an acre of his Blairsville land to Parr (Clarke County Deed Book BB, page 312). The address for the Parr's lot was 1689 South Lumpkin Street, the present address for Five Points Village and home of Earth Fare and Add Drug Store. In the U.S. Census records, Parr is identified as a house painter, but some early editions of the *Athens City Directory* report that he also operated a grocery store at 1687 South Milledge Avenue, which was next door to his home.

Very little information is available on Blairsville, but this Athens suburb is mentioned in more than 25 Athens newspaper articles between 1883 and 1911. Blairsville apparently was a lively community of several families, with an active Church and Sunday School, and a Good Templars Lodge. From various newspaper articles from 1883 to 1911, it was learned that in addition to the

Blairs, other families living in the community were Bone, Gean, Lilly, Mabry, Parr, Westmoreland, and Woods. Because the city limits of Athens were very near the Blair property, most of the other residents of Blairsville were identified as being just outside or just beyond the city limits. The community existed until at least 1911 when the last reference found for it was in the obituary of Miss Dorcas Bone that was published in the *Athens Banner*, August 24, 1911.

Brooklyn Branch—See **Brooklyn Community**.

Brooklyn Cemetery is a nine-acre burial ground located behind Holy Cross Evangelical Lutheran Church at 800 West Lake Drive in the heart of the old Brooklyn Community, where several hundred African-Americans are buried.

Brooklyn Community is an important part of early Athens history and very little has been written about it—and some of that is incorrect. The exact boundaries of Brooklyn Community are not known, but it was located in the vicinity of what was then the end of West Broad Street about where present-day Alps Road and Hawthorne Avenue intersect with West Broad. On W. W. Thomas' 1874 map of Athens, the community is shown as being entirely on the south side of West Broad Street, but in more modern times a small neighborhood on the north side of West Broad Street along Hawthorne Avenue is considered to be part of the Brooklyn Community. One of Athens' African-American schools was located in an African-American church in Brooklyn Community. For a very short time during the Spanish-American War (1898), a U.S. Army camp (Camp Haskell) was located nearby between Cobb Street and West Broad Street, and some modern investigators erroneously concluded that there must have been some soldiers stationed at Camp Haskell who were from the famous Brooklyn Borough of New York who gave the community its name. But they were mistaken. The Brooklyn Community existed long before that time. The first reference found for the community is on W. W. Thomas' 1874 map of Athens. A brief article in the January 18, 1881, issue of the *Athens Banner* also mentioned a resident of the community. It also was identified in the March 2, 1882, *Banner Watchman* as follows: "Brooklyn, a large colored village near the city, speaks of incorporating." Brooklyn Branch courses through the area, and the first reference found about this stream was in the *Banner Watchman*, October 23, 1883. On Thomas' 1874 map, Brooklyn Branch is identified as Phinizy Branch. The stream flows under present-day Fortson Drive and West Lake Drive. (See Fig. 12).

Camp Haskell was one of several U.S. Army camps established in Georgia and South Carolina during and just after the end of the Spanish-American War (April 1898-June 1898) to provide a base of operations for U.S. soldiers destined for the occupation of Cuba. Camp Haskell was located in western Athens on a tract of land fronting on Cobb Street that extended southwesterly toward present-day West Broad Street. The location was identified in an article in the *Athens Banner* dated November 18, 1898, as being "between the residence of Mr. J. S. King [749 Cobb Street] and the old Phinizy place." The "Phinizy place" can be identified on Thomas' 1874 map of Athens as the large undeveloped tract labeled "Ferdinand Phinizy." It is bordered on the east side by Billups Street and on the southeast by Phinizy Street, which is the southwestern end of present-day Hancock Avenue. On the western boundary was a tract labeled as the property of Lamar Cobb. (See Fig. 18).

The camp was named for Brig. Gen. Joseph Theodore Haskell

(1838-1898) from Ohio, who was a member of the Seventeeth U.S. Infantry, one of the units that fought in the Spanish-American War. Haskell died on September 16, 1898, from wounds received in the Battle of Santiago on July 1, 1898, and is buried in Arlington National Cemetery. Plans were for Camp Haskell to accommodate from 5,000 to 10,000 soldiers, and it was estimated that they would contribute as much as $100,000 per month to the local economy. Athens lobbied heavily to have the camp located here, and numerous businesses and individuals contributed money to the effort in order to provide a rent-free property for the camp and free electricity and water. In an article dated September 23, 1898, the *Weekly Banner* reported that 46 donors had pledged from $10 to $300 each for a total of $2,100. The article speculated that when the local railroads overcame the red tape associated with such an endeavor and made their donations, the total would easily reach $5,000.

Camp Haskell was commanded by Brig. Gen. George Morton Randall (1841-1918). Randall joined the U.S. Army at the beginning of the War Between the States in April 1861 and retired in 1905 after 44 years of service. The November 3, 1898, issue of the *Athens Daily Banner* reported that the parade grounds of Camp Haskell would be located on the Mitchell Bridge Road (later named Oglethorpe Avenue) in front of the residence of Mr. William Shrewsbury Holman (632 Oglethorpe Avenue), and the Athens Street Railway would extend its tracks to that site. (See Fig. 22).

The first soldiers to occupy Camp Haskell were the Fifteenth Pennsylvania regiment and a portion of the Third New Jersey regiment, who arrived on November 17, 1898. (See Fig. 19 and 20). The Two Hundred and Second New York volunteers came in the next day. These first arrivals totaled about 3,200 soldiers, but the number increased with the arrival of the remainder of the Third New Jersey regiment. The November 25, 1898, *Weekly Banner* reported that there were "exactly 4,268 enlisted men and officers" at Camp Haskell. Soon after establishment of the camp, construction was begun on six buildings, viz. an administration/hospital building, two sick wards, a "nursery" for convalescents, a kitchen, and a mess hall. Wooden platforms were constructed throughout the camp to accommodate the tents used by the soldiers so no one had to sleep on the ground.

There were constant rumors from the beginning that all the soldiers at Camp Haskell would soon be shipped to Cuba and the camp would be deserted. This finally did occur; and, after less than three months of use, the last soldiers moved out of Camp Haskell on February 11, 1899. Soon after the camp was vacated, the February 24, 1899, issue of the *Weekly Banner* carried the news that at ten o'clock Saturday morning, March 4, 1899, all of the buildings and equipment left at Camp Haskell would be sold for cash to the highest bidders. This included the six main buildings, eight water closets, two bath tubs, 51 latrines, 24 cook houses, six wooden shacks, two stables, 591 wooden tent floors, and a variety of other items. It was speculated that the city would buy the main hospital building and convert it into a school house for African-American children because their school on Broad Street was overcrowded.

The Camp Haskell in Athens was created for white soldiers, and there was a Camp Haskell in Macon constructed for black soldiers.

Camp Wilkins is described on page 38 in the book *A Post Card History of Athens, Georgia* as follows: "Camp Wilkins was a large wooden and stucco structure built in 1924 on the former farmland of the John J. Wilkins family on present-day Ag Drive. One of its original functions was to accommodate summer 4-H campers. It also served various other needs of the university, including housing for students in financial straits. When the U.S. Navy Pre-Flight Training School occupied part of the UGA campus during World War II, Camp Wilkins served as a dormitory for the trainees. In the early 1960s, at the heigth of the Cold War and the universal fear of The Bomb, the Psychology Department used rooms in Camp Wilkins adapted to simulate bomb shelters in order to study human behavior under such circumstances. Camp Wilkins was leveled in 1964 to make way for the Driftmier Agriculture Engineering Center, named for Rudolph Henry Driftmier (1898-1979), former Head of the Department of Agricultural Engineering."

Carr's Hill was established by William Anthony Carr (1796-1872), an early settler in the Athens area. He owned 1,242½ acres on the east side of the North Oconee River that was "sold" to him for $10.00 by his father, Thomas Carr, on September 15, 1820 (Clarke County Deed Book L, page 452). The property included most of present-day East Athens. Daniel W. Easley previously sold this property to William Low who died before paying Easley for the property, and Thomas Carr bought the 1,242½ acres at a sheriff's auction on April 1, 1817, for $1,756.00 (Clarke County Deed Book L, page 117). William Carr built his home on the highest elevation of the hill shortly after his marriage to Cynthia Walker in 1817, and many people over time have referred to his home, not the property, as Carr's Hill.

Cloverhurst Farm—See **Cloverhurst Avenue** in the streets list.

Cobbham is a residential tract developed by John Addison Cobb (1783-1855) when he subdivided his farm on the north side of

Athens in 1834 and advertised 80 lots for sale. This was Athens' first suburb. The correct pronunciation is "Cobb Ham." The earliest allusions to the community refer to it as the Village of Cobbham, and it has always been considered a prestigious location to live. The original boundaries of the neighborhood were (approximately) Prince Avenue (then called Federal Road), Meigs Street, and Rocksprings Street (See Fig. 1). These boundaries have remained somewhat fluid over the years. Milton Leathers said that in the 1980s he heard John Bondurant say that the boundaries of Cobbham were wherever Dr. Phinizy Spalding wanted them to be! The first reference found for Cobbham was in the *Southern Banner*, March 9, 1839.

Cord Mill Community is the name of an area derived from the Mallison Braided Cord Company (later named Puritan Cordage Mills—Mallison Division), which manufactured thread, string, twine, and rope. The mill was built in 1896 at the site of the old Pioneer Paper Mill at the junction of Barber Creek and McNutt Creek just off U.S. Highway 441, south of Athens. The facility has always been called the Cord Mill, and the residential and business community that grew up around the mill also is known by that name. The mill closed about 1992 and moved its operation to Madison, Georgia. The building remained empty since that time and was gutted by a devastating fire in 2016. The first reference found regarding the Cord Mill was in the *Weekly Banner*, March 31, 1899.

Five Points is a well-known Athens landmark created in 1913 when Milledge Circle was cut through to join the intersection of Lumpkin Street and Milledge Avenue. Prior to 1913, the community was called Blairsville (See Fig. 2). The first reference found for

Athens Streets & Neighborhoods

Five Points was in the *Banner-Herald*, June 6, 1926. See Blairsville in the list of neighborhoods.

Fowler's Junction is the point where the Gainesville Midland Railroad track branches off from the Seaboard Airline Railroad track on the east side of Prince Avenue just north of the junction of Prince Avenue and Oglethorpe Avenue. It is in the immediate vicinity of the community of Fowler Town or Fowler's Town.

Fowler Town or **Fowler's Town** was an African-American community on the northwestern side of town. The first reference found for Fowler Town was in the *Athens Banner*, May 13, 1910. According to a later article in the *Banner-Herald*, April 11, 1926, Fowler's Town was located "…just beyond the Normal School District." Fowler Town apparently received its name due to the large number of people named Fowler who lived in the area. Thomas C. Fowler ran a store on Prince Avenue Extension in the vicinity of the State Normal School. Fowler and his sons Charles M., J. Clifton, Thomas C., and Walter H. all lived on Prince Avenue Extension. A David Fowler and Julian Fowler also had addresses on Prince Avenue Extension. Furthermore, several other Fowlers lived on Prince Avenue before it reached the city limits where the name became Prince Avenue Extension, including Carl C., Ernest C., John A., Maude L., Ruby I. and William A. According to the April 11, 1926, article in the *Banner-Herald*, "A number of colored women of Athens have recently been organizing themselves into groups which are doing a great deal toward improving health conditions among the needy members of their race." The article further stated that "…twenty-one women of Fowler's Town…organized a club for the purpose of giving aid to the sick and poverty-stricken. The group…has furnished necessities continually to some individuals or families in distress. It supplies bedding and linen to the sick, nurses those who are unable to pay for professional service, washes their clothes, and even keeps house for them until they are able to take care of themselves again...So much good has this club accomplished that other colored communities are making arrangements to organize similar groups. Thursday afternoon a meeting of a large number of Negro women was held at the Athens High and Industrial School and another of these charitable clubs was formed. Two nurses connected with the Athens Red Cross addressed the meeting, offering splendid suggestions to the club members concerning their activities. The talks proved very helpful and instructive and were greatly appreciated by all present. The movement on the part of the Negro women is indicative of their keen desire to help the progress and improvement of their race."

Granite Row (also called **Granite Range**) was a block of buildings on the south side of Front Street (later Broad Street) between Spring Street and South Jackson Street. Early on, it often was called Granite Range. Some of Athens finest merchants had their businesses on Granite Row, and they had many ads in the Athens newspapers from the 1840s to at least 1879. Addresses listed in the ads ranged from No. 1 Granite Row to No. 10 Granite Row. In his book *Confederate Athens*, Kenneth Coleman included a map (p. 215) prepared by Charles A. Rowland, IV that shows the area, and some of the businesses listed have ads in the contemporary newspapers identifying their addresses as Granite Row. The first reference found for Granite Row was in the *Southern Whig*, December 7, 1844, and the first reference found for Granite Range was the *Southern Whig*, February 13, 1845. (See Fig. 14).

Athens Streets & Neighborhoods

Happy Top was a mill village associated with the Southern Manufacturing Company, a cotton mill located on the western side of North Chase Street. The cotton mill opened in January 1903. I learned the origin of the name of Happy Top from *Athens Memories, The WPA Federal Writers' Project Interviews*, edited by Al Hester. The neighborhood was so named as a result of a conversation between two residents, Lelia Bramblett (1878-1954) and a young man she encountered on the Chase Street bridge that spans the railroad track. He asked her where she was going, and she said "To the Holiness Meeting." He said, "To get happy?" She answered, "And stay all night." From that conversation, the area became known as Happy Top. Mrs. Bramblett added, "It was kinda a rough place, too." My father, Walter Lafayette Doster (1915-1989), told me about it when I was a youngster. He said the mill workers considered the neighborhood around the mill to be "theirs," and outsiders were not welcome. Folks who did not work at the mill or live in the area did not dare enter the space for fear of being physically attacked.

Hot Corner is the name of the intersection of Hull and Washington streets. Historically, most of the businesses in the vicinity of this intersection have long been owned by African-Americans. Central to the community was the Morton Theater, built in 1910 by Monroe Bowers "Pink" Morton (1856-1919). A great deal of information has been published on the history of the Morton Theater and the many other black-owned businesses in this area. A Hot Corner Celebration & Soul Food Festival is held here each year on the second Saturday in June.

Jackson Street Cemetery is often referred to as Old Athens Cemetery. This was the first public cemetery in Athens and served from the time Athens was founded until after Oconee Hill Cemetery was opened in 1856. It is located on the east side of South Jackson Street between the University of Georgia's Art Museum on the north side and Baldwin Hall on the south side. (See Fig. 8). There are about 180 graves identified with tombstones or other markers, and the identities of more than 50 other individuals buried there are known but they have no markers. In addition, there are hundreds of unmarked graves that fill the entire site. A great deal of information on this cemetery is available on pages 17–43 in *Athens-Clarke County, Georgia Cemeteries*, edited by Eve B. Weeks for the Athens Historical Society and published in 1999.

Lickskillet was a trendy neighborhood where many prominent Athenians proudly lived in the mid and late 1800s. The community was bounded by Clayton, Hoyt, and Jackson streets and the North Oconee River. This area includes the present-day Hotel Indigo, the Athens-Clarke County Fire Station No. 1, and the Ware-Lyndon House. The area behind Lickskillet and extending across the North Oconee River was inhabited by poorer Athens black families, and this territory also was called Lickskillet.

Lilly Park was a planned development in 1889 that never materialized. It was to be on the east side of South Milledge Avenue, just south of Five Points. The venture was to be sited on 112 acres of undeveloped land formerly owned by Edward Lilly " ... at the end of South Milledge Avenue" in the approximate vicinity of present-day Morton Avenue, University Drive, Pinecrest Drive, and other streets in that neighborhood. Advertisements for the park and residential development began in the July 16, 1889, issue of the *Athens Banner* [Weekly]. The plan was to build a city park surrounded by expensive houses, and developers planned to have the Athens streetcar route extended out to the area. The endeavor soon failed, and the park was never built. However, the area eventually was developed as an upscale residential neighborhood that remains today.

Lynwood Park is a residential section adjacent to Cobbham that was developed by the West Virginia Land Company in 1906. The tract is more than 30 acres in size and is bounded by Billups, Cobb, and Hillcrest streets and Hancock Avenue. There is a plat of the property in Clarke County Deed Book 1 on pages 579, 580, 581-A, and 581-B.

Morristown was a small, compact African-American neighborhood apparently bounded somewhat by Prince Avenue, Chase Street, The Boulevard, and Morris Street (now Lyndon Avenue). Within these boundaries also were Cain Street, Cherry Street (now DuBose Avenue), and Cohen Street. Apparently, most or all of the houses in the Morristown neighborhood consisted of rental property owned by some prominent members of the Athens Jewish community. According to a legal notice in the *Weekly Banner*, March 25, 1898, regarding the estate of former Athenian Rosa C. Stern Jacobson, she owned eight houses on Morris Street and four houses on Cherry Street (Dubose Avenue). Also see Morris Street.

Newtown is a twelve-square-block African-American neighborhood developed in the early 1890s in North Athens between Barber Street and the North Oconee River. (See Fig. 10). The other major streets in the neighborhood were Athens Avenue, Atlanta Avenue, Augusta Avenue, Bird Street, Macon Avenue, and Savannah Street. Most of these streets still exist. A school for black children was established in the neighborhood in 1911. The first reference found for Newtown was in the *Weekly Banner*, August 22, 1893.

Normal Heights was an early name for Normaltown that originated soon after the State Normal School was established in Athens in 1892. In an article in the [Athens] *Banner-Herald* on August 6, 1922, newspaper publisher T. Larry Gantt credited William Shrewsbury Holman with championing the area and said that Holman was personally responsible for much of the development of the neighborhood. Gantt referred to the area as the "Druid Hills" of Athens, comparing it to a fashionable residential section of Atlanta. The suburb sometimes was referred to simply as "The Heights," which also was the name of William Holman's home on Oglethorpe Avenue. (See Fig. 22). Also see Normaltown.

Normaltown is the community comprised of residences and commercial and private businesses in the vicinity of the old State Normal School property on the northern end of Prince Avenue. There is a description and history of this area on pages 97-106 of *A Post Card History of Athens, Georgia*, published by The Athens Historical Society in 2002. The name "Normal School" comes from a French term *'ecole normale*, meaning to serve as a model. The first known use of this expression in the United States was by famous educator Horace Mann in Boston in 1839. The old Normal School property now is occupied by the University of Georgia's Athens campus of the Medical College of Georgia. Also see Normal Heights.

Oconee Heights is sited in the northwestern part of Athens-Clarke County on the Jefferson Road (Highway 129 North), not far from the boundary with Jackson County. Oconee Heights was the name of the 293-acre farm in that area owned by Christian

Frederick Auslund (1862-1921). Auslund's middle name also has been seen spelled as Fredrich. The farm was established in 1902 when Auslund bought 202 acres from James S. King and Sarah C. King on March 17, 1902 (Clarke County Deed Book VV, pages 312-313), then added another 91 acres he bought from Louis Nichols on April 1, 1902 (Clarke County Deed Book UU, pages 391-392). (See Fig. 17).

Auslund's farm was located on both sides of Highway 129 at the intersection of the present-day Jefferson River Road and extended up the west side of Jefferson River Road to the old Boggs Chapel Methodist Church. After Boggs Chapel moved to a new location, the old church building was occupied by Gateway Methodist Church; at present the facilities are home to Athens Latino Mission United Methodist Church.

According to an article in the [Athens] *Banner* on September 18, 1903, Auslund grew very little cotton on his farm, but mostly produced wheat and forage crops. He also maintained a 20-acre peach orchard stocked mostly with Elberta peach trees. Auslund's main interests were raising registered Holstein-Friesian cattle for milk production, registered Cotswold sheep for wool and meat, Cheshire White hogs for meat, and fine registered horses.

Auslund was quite a "man of the world." He was born in Sundsvall, Sweden, in August 1862. After graduating from the University of Gotenburg, Auslund spent some time living in England, France, and Germany, where he mastered a number of languages, before moving to St. Paul, Minnesota, in 1882. He soon returned to Sweden for a short stay before moving back to the United States where he settled in Chicago for a short while. Fred Auslund became a naturalized U.S. citizen on November 13, 1884. From Chicago he went to Louisiana and was engaged in the sawmill business for several years. While living in Louisiana, Fred Auslund married Anna Clark (1865-1950) from Burlington, Iowa. Anna also is listed in the census records as being a native of Illinois. Two daughters and two sons were born to the Auslunds in Louisiana. From there, the Auslunds moved to Maryland, where Fred entered the law profession with the brother of an ex-governor of Pennsylvania. Auslund practiced law in Maryland for several years, then moved to Florida in 1901 and became a member of the Florida Bar. After living in Florida for a year, the Auslunds moved to Athens. The Auslunds added two more daughters to their family once they moved to Georgia.

At Oconee Heights, Auslund built an eleven-room house fashioned after the houses in Southern California, which was unlike any other house in Clarke County. It had all the modern conveniences. He even had a long-distance telephone installed in the house, which was an unusual luxury at that time. On September 2, 1909, Auslund sold his Oconee Heights home and farm to Alexander Stephens Rhodes (1861-1923), and Rhodes sold his home in Lynwood Park in Athens to Auslund. The 1903 newspaper article stated that Fred Auslund was so satisfied with living in Athens that he intended to spend the rest of his life here; however, he eventually succumbed to his inherent wanderlust, and in January 1912, C. Fred Auslund and his family relocated to Florida. In the 1920 census, Fred and Anna Auslund and their two youngest daughters are identified as living in Boca Grande, Florida, and Fred's occupation was given as ex-railroad agent. Fred Auslund died in 1921. Anna lived another 29 years and died in 1950 at age 85. Fred and Anna are buried in Pineland Cemetery in Sebring, Florida.

A 1908 survey plat of Oconee Heights shows four named streets on that part of Auslund's property located on the north side of Highway 129: Auslund Avenue, Nichols Street (previously

School Street), Rhodes Street, and School Street (previously Church Street). There can be no doubt that Auslund Avenue was named for C. Fred Auslund, Nichols Street was named for local merchant and farmer Louis Harrison Nichols (1856-1918), and Rhodes Street was named for A. S. Rhodes, who bought Auslund's house in 1909. School Street led to a 24 X 40-foot, two-room school house built in 1907. In June 1924, articles in the [Athens] *Banner-Herald* announced plans for a fund raiser for a new high school to be built in the Oconee Heights community, but there is no evidence that it was ever constructed. Nichols Street no longer exists, but it appears that present-day Ambler Road now traverses part of the former route of Auslund Avenue and Rhodes Street. School Street still exists as a narrow, unpaved, nearly impassable alley. There is no trace of Auslund's eleven-room mansion.

Old Athens Cemetery—see **Jackson Street Cemetery.**

Princeton Community now is an upscale residential community where some of Athens' finest homes and condominiums have been built in recent years. The community is roughly bounded by the Middle Oconee River on the West, South Lumpkin Street on the East, and the Macon Highway (441/15) on the South. In 1833, Camak Manufacturing Company was incorporated on the eastern side of the Middle Oconee River, but before the mill went into operation in 1835, the name was changed to Princeton Factory. For many years a question has existed regarding the origin of the name of this community. One component maintains that it was named for the Prince Family who owned the land before the factory was built, while others say that it was named for Princeton, New Jersey. There are valid arguments for both sides. On January 17, 1824, Noah Prince, John Prince, Noah F. Prince, and Garland

W. Prince bought 683 acres of land that includes this area, built a grist mill that carried their name, and the nearby bridge across the Middle Oconee River was called Prince's Bridge. The senior member of the family, Noah Prince, Sr. (c.1761-1836), was a veteran of the Revolutionary War. The Princes later sold the land to a group of businessmen who built the factory. It is claimed by some that the community that grew up around the factory was called Prince Town, later shortened to Princeton. The first reference found for Princeton in Clarke County was in the *Southern Banner*, December 20, 1834, in a legal notice announcing that the name of Camak Manufacturing Company had been changed to Princeton Factory. In more modern times, Oscar Williford Haygood operated a grist mill at the site from the 1940s into the late 1950s.

Pulaski Heights — See **Pulaski Heights** under street names.

Rutherford — See **Bob Godfrey Road.**

Six-Mile Station — An early name for **Winterville** (see below).

White City was a small mill village on Inglewood Avenue in East Athens around the White City Manufacturing Company founded in 1909 by J. W. Ingle and J. T. Jordan. The mill was created to produce cotton and wool "…thread, yarn, cloth, roping, twine, and anything else into which either cotton or wool can be manufactured." In its short life, however, the Ingle and Jordan company manufactured only thread and yarn. In 1919, the Union Thread Company of Cincinnati bought the mill with the intention of doubling its capacity within the first year. The mill changed hands again in 1922 when O. W. Bowen, M. B. Crews, and W. W. Crews of Jewell, Georgia, bought the factory, and they, too, announced that they intended to double the output of the mill and planned to triple the number of employees, which was 30 when they made the purchase. They also announced that in addition to yarn, they planned to produce finished cloth. The mill was sold again in November 1926 to E. E. Hendrix of Dallas County, Alabama, B. M. Graves of Mecklenburg County, North Carolina, and Claude Ramsaur of Greenville County, South Carolina. These new owners changed the name of the establishment to Clarke Cotton Mills and announced that their business was the "...manufacturing, selling, and dealing in cotton goods and products of every kind and character, the owning and dealing in real estate, machinery, and the operation of manufacturing plants of any and all kinds and character pertaining to manufactured products, whether made from cotton, wool, or any and all other material, and such other business or businesses as may be incidental thereto." Clarke Cotton Mills did not last long, and less than a year after having their charter approved, they also went under, and after only 18 years and four owners, the mill was no more. The legal announcement in the *Banner-Herald* stated that on the "first Tuesday in August 1927, before the Court House door...all the land, buildings, machinery, and other property belonging to the mill would be sold to the highest and best bidder." Also see Inglewood Avenue for additional information.

Whitehall community is located in the south-central part of the county and is bisected by the North Oconee River near its confluence with the Middle Oconee River, which is the county line between Clarke and Oconee counties. Whitehall takes its name from the home of John White (1799-1889), who came here from Larne, County Antrim, Ireland in 1837 to manage the Georgia Factory. The factory was originally known as Athens Manufacturing

Company. This was the first cotton mill in the South operated by water power when it was built in 1830 by Athens businessmen Augustin Smith Clayton (1783-1839), William Dearing (1785-1853), John Nisbet (1781-1841), and Abram Walker. White later bought the factory and became wealthy as it grew and prospered. In his later years White was regarded as one of the richest men in Georgia. In 1854, he replaced the original frame building with a modern brick structure. This building was destroyed by fire in 1892, and a new brick building was erected that still stands. This old factory building was converted to apartments in 1997. White built a home in the community that he named White Hall. In 1891, White's son John Richards White (1847-1919) dismantled his father's original house and rebuilt it in Dillard, Georgia. John R. White then built a magnificent Victorian mansion in its place that was designed by Athens architect William Winstead Thomas (1849-1904). The younger White's house still stands and is owned by the University of Georgia's Warnell School of Forestry and Natural Resources, along with more than two thousand acres of land behind it.

Wilkins, Camp — see **Camp Wilkins**.

Winters or **Winter's Station** — See **Winterville**.

Winterville or **Winter Ville** exists because of the railroad, like many other towns throughout the United States. As trains traveled across the country, there was a need for a constant supply of water and wood or coal at regular intervals to keep the steam engines running. Consequently, many new towns were created along the route to furnish that need, as well as providing a depot for the convenience of passengers and for shipping and receiving freight.

Athens Streets & Neighborhoods

The settlement was first known as Six-Mile Station, because it was six miles by rail from Athens. According to an article in the *Banner-Watchman* dated February 23, 1883, the town was renamed for John Winter (1833-1886), who was born in Germany and came to Athens in 1859 to work for the railroad. He also was engaged in farming and operated a merchantile store near the depot. Other members of the Winter family also came from Germany, and some of them also worked for the railraod. The name was changed to Winterville in 1866 when a U.S. post office was established here, and John Winter was hired as the first postmaster. This first post office was located in John Winter's mercantile store near his home, which was located at 149 South Georgia Avenue. The name of the depot and the community also were sometimes called Winters and Winter's Station. When Winterville was incorporated in 1904, the county line between Clarke and Oglethorpe counties divided the town. Two years later, in 1906, the state legislature allowed the citizens to vote on what county they wanted to be in. They chose Clarke, and the county line was moved accordingly. The first reference found for Six-Mile Station was in the *Southern Banner* on March 11, 1863. The first reference found for Winterville was in the *Southern Banner* on July 3, 1867. No reference to Winter Ville was found in any newspaper, but Winter V. was used on an 1874 Georgia map. Also, neither Winters nor Winter's Station were found in any Athens newspaper, but the station was labeled Winters on Georgia maps in 1885 and 1895, and Winter's Sta. on an 1899 Georgia map.

References

Most of these references contain further information regarding the people for whom some Athens streets and neighborhoods were named.

From the Athens Historic Newspapers Archive posted online by The Digital Library of Georgia: (http://athnewspapers.galileo.usg.edu/athnewspapers-j2k/search)

Athenian,	1827-1832
Athens Herald,	1913-1923
Clarke County Courier,	1903-1913
Southern Banner,	1832-1882
Southern Watchman,	1855-1882
Southern Whig/Southern Herald,	1838-1850
Daily/Weekly Banner-Watchman,	1882-1889
Daily/Weekly Athens Banner,	1889-1922
Athens Banner-Herald,	1923-1928

Gary L. Doster

Aldridge, Dan A., Jr. *To Lasso the Clouds, The Beginning of Aviation in Georgia.* Mercer University Press, Macon, GA, 2016.

Athens City Directory. Various issues from 1889 onward.

Boney, F. N. *A Pictorial History of the University of Georgia.* Athens: The University of Georgia Press, 1984, second edition 2000.

Brooks, Robert Preston. *The University of Georgia Under Sixteen Administrations 1785-1955.* Athens: The University of Georgia Press, 1956.

Coleman, Kenneth. *Confederate Athens.* Athens: The University of Georgia Press, 1967.

Coleman, Kenneth and Charles Stephen Gurr. *Dictionary of Georgia Biography,* Volume One and Volume Two. Athens: The University of Georgia Press, 1983.

Coleman, Kenneth, Numan V. Bartley, William F. Holmes, F. N. Boney, Phinizy Spalding, and Charles E. Wynes. *A History of Georgia.* Athens: The University of Georgia Press, 1977.

Coulter, E. Merton. *Georgia, A Short History.* Fourth Printing, 1973. Chapel Hill: The University of North Carolina Press.

Coulter, E. Merton. *College Life in the Old South.* Third Printing, 1973. Athens: The University of Georgia Press, 1973.

Doster, Emily Jean and Gary L. Doster. *Athens.* Charleston, SC: Arcadia Publishing, 2011.

Athens Streets & Neighborhoods

Doster, Gary L. *Post Card History of Athens, Georgia*. Athens: The Athens Historical Society, 2002.

Dyer, Thomas G. *The University of Georgia: A Bicentennial History 1785-1985*. Athens: The University of Georgia Press, 1985.

Foley, Emma and Mary Quinn. *Winterville, Georgia: A Classic Railroad Town*. Winterville, GA: Emma Foley and Mary Quinn, 2014.

Gagnon, Michael J. *Transition to an Industrial South, Athens, Georgia, 1830-1870*. Baton Rouge: Louisiana State University Press, 2012.

Hester, Al, ed. *Athens Memories, The WPA Federal Writers' Project Interviews*. Athens: The Green Berry Press, 2001.

Hester, Conoly. *Athens, Georgia: Celebrating 200 Years at the Millennium*. Corporate Profiles by Al Hester, Photographs by Terry Allen. Sponsored by the Athens-Clarke Heritage Foundation, Inc. Montgomery: Community Communications, Inc., 1999.

Hicks, Paul DeForest. *Joseph Henry Lumpkin, Georgia's First Chief Justice*. Athens: The University of Georgia Press, 2002.

Hull, Augustus Longstreet. *Annals of Athens, Georgia 1801-1901*. Athens: Banner Job Office, 1906. Third Edition, Athens: Heritage Papers, 2014.

Hynds, Ernest. *Antebellum Athens and Clarke County Georgia*. Athens: The University of Georgia Press, 1974.

Marshall, Charlotte Thomas. *Oconee Hill Cemetery of Athens, Georgia*, Vol. I. Athens: The Athens Historical Society, 2009.

Marshall, Charlotte Thomas, ed. *Historic Houses of Athens, Georgia*. Athens: The Athens Historical Society, 1987.

Marshall, Charlotte Thomas, ed. *The Tangible Past in Athens, Georgia*. Athens: Charlotte Thomas Marshall, 2014.

Reap, James. *Athens, A Pictorial History*. Norfolk, VA: The Donning Company, 1982.

Rowe, H. J. *History of Athens and Clarke County*. Athens: The McGregor Co., 1923. Reprinted by Southern Historical Press, Inc. Greenville, SC, 2000.

Thomas, Frances Taliaferro. *A Portrait of Historic Athens and Clarke* County. Athens: The University of Georgia Press, 1992.

Mathis, Ray, ed. *"Uncle Tom" Reed's Memoir of the University of Georgia*. University of Georgia Libraries, Miscellanea Publications, No. 11. Athens: The University of Georgia Libraries, 1974.

Weeks, Eve B., ed. *Athens-Clarke County Georgia Cemeteries*. Athens: The Athens Historical Society, 1999.

Illustrations

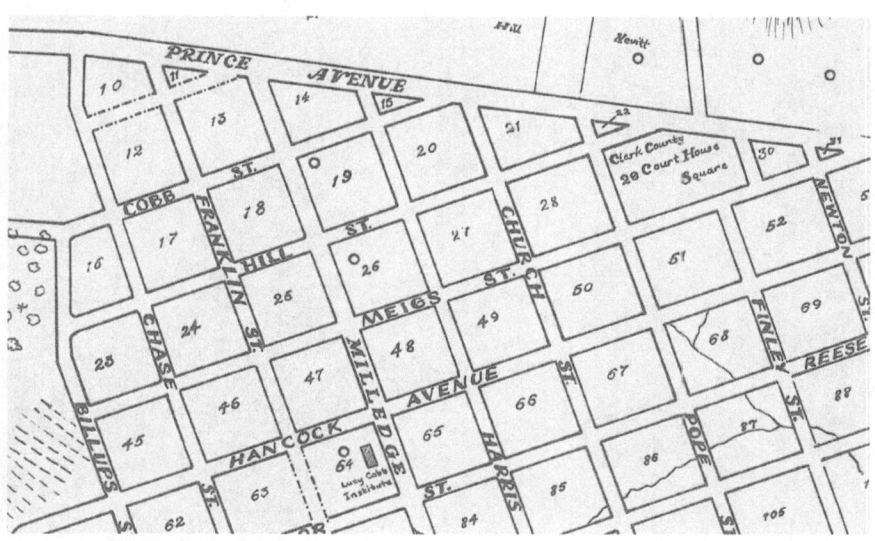

Figure 1. The Village of Cobbham was a triangular-shaped neighborhood originally bordered on the north by Prince Avenue and on the south by Meigs Street. This view is from Thomas's 1874 map of Athens.

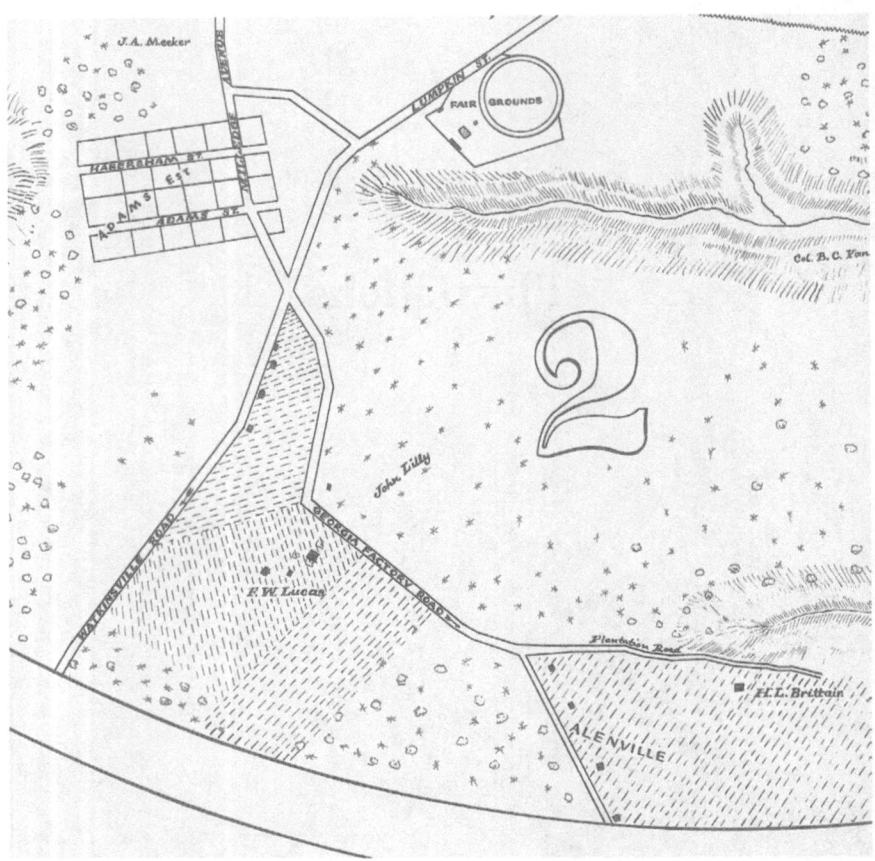

Figure 2. This section of Thomas' 1874 map shows several interesting Athens features that have been altered dramatically. The Athens Fairgrounds on Lumpkin Street is now the location of UGA's Forrest "Spec" Towns track, Butts-Mehre Heritage Hall, and the UGA Athletic Ticket Office. (cont. on next page)

Athens Streets & Neighborhoods

The subdivision on Milledge Avenue identified as Adams Estate apparently was not developed until much later, and it appears that Adams Street was renamed Woodlawn Avenue and Habersham Street is now Oakland Avenue.

This also shows the intersection of Lumpkin Street and Milledge Avenue before Milledge Circle was developed to join the intersection in 1913 to create our present Five Points. Until then, this intersection was known as Blairsville. As this community extended down Lumpkin Street toward Princeton, Lumpkin Street was called Watkinsville Road. And as one traveled South on Milledge Avenue (called Georgia Factory Road on Thomas' map), the black neighborhood named Allenville (misspelled as Alenville on Thomas' map) was located a few blocks south of present-day Five Points, where the road forked near the present-day intersection of Milledge Avenue, East Campus Drive, and Annes Court.

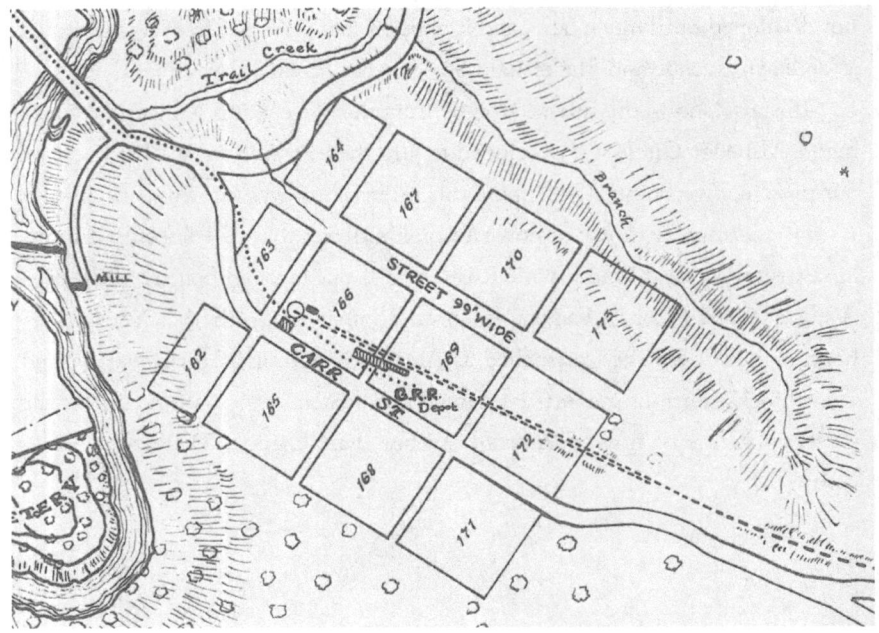

From W. W. Thomas' 1874 map

Figure 3. On Thomas' 1874 map, what is shown as Carr Street is present-day Oconee Street, and the street identified as "Street 99' Wide" is now Oak Street. The track of the Georgia Railroad originally came to a dead end between Carr Street and Street 99' Wide in 1840 as shown here.

Athens Streets & Neighborhoods

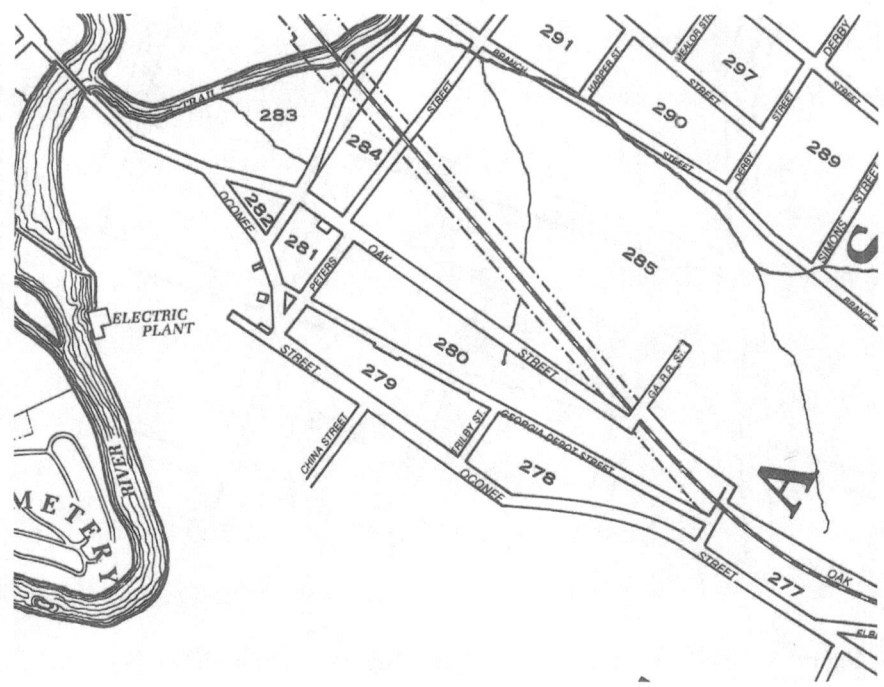

From Barnett's 1895 map

Figure 4. Barnett's 1895 map shows that when the track was diverted to cross Trail Creek and the Oconee River in 1882, the old track bed became Georgia Depot Street. In 1957, the residents along Georgia Depot Street petitioned the city to change the name of the street to Georgia Drive.

Figure 5. On Barnett's 1895 map, States Rights Street is shown connecting Milledge Avenue and Church Street. Harris Street is shown to the North. The name of States Rights Street was changed to Henderson Avenue in 1897.

Figure 6. Shown here on Barnett's 1895 map, Phinizy Street is thought to have been named for Ferdinand Phinizy and Bowdre Street, Jacob Street, Leonard Street, and Stewart Street likely were named for four of his sons. None of these streets exist by these names today.

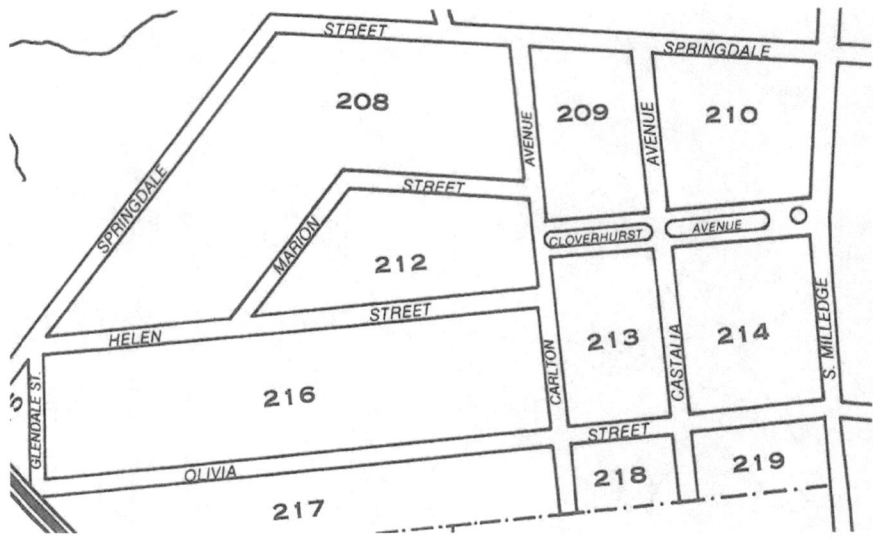

Figure 7. On Barnett's 1895 map of Athens, Helen, Marion, and Olivia streets shown here were named for the daughters of Dr. Henry Hull Carlton and his wife, Helen, who developed the neighborhood. The present area does not exactly conform to the layout on Barnett's map, and these streets are not located here by those names, but Olivia Street may be the present site of Rutherford Street.

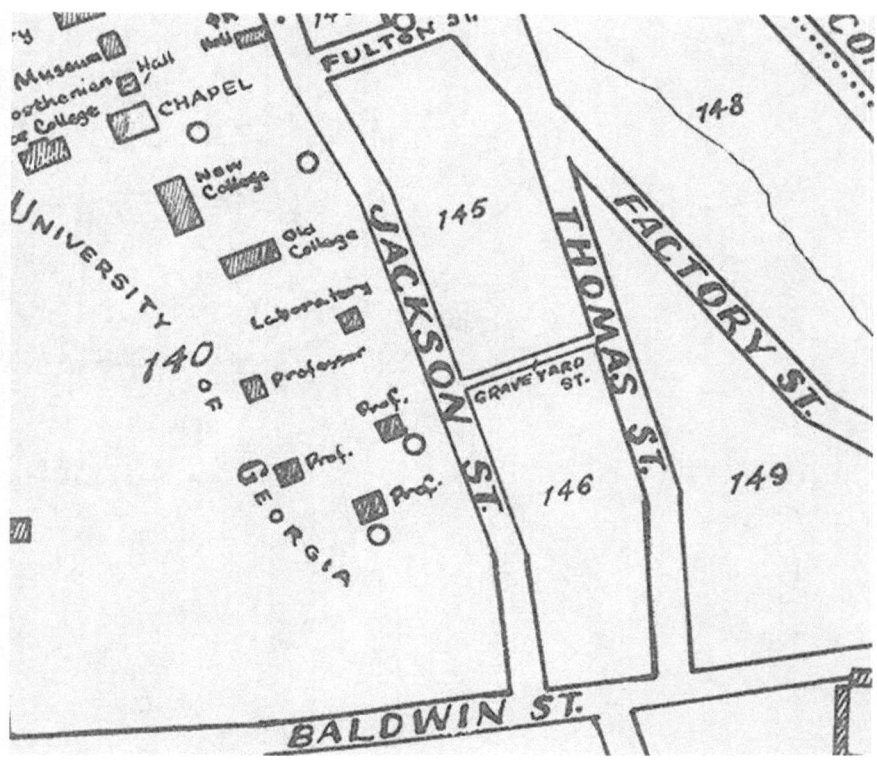

Figure 8. Jackson Street Cemetery is shown on Thomas' 1874 map as lot 146, and it extends from Graveyard Street all the way to Baldwin Street. Prior to being named Graveyard Street, the street was named Brown Street. After Graveyard Street, it became Magazine Street.

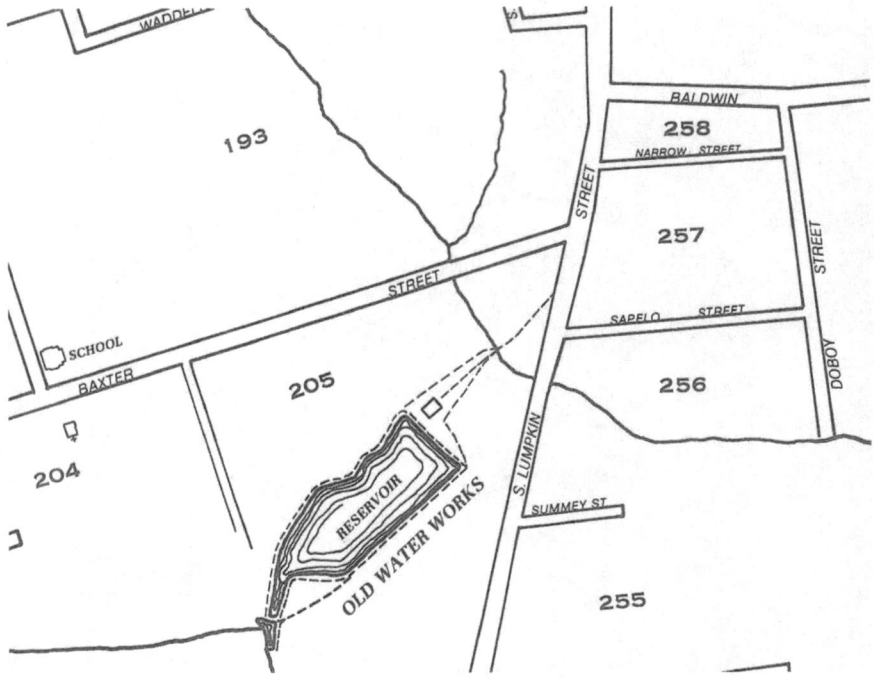

Figure 9. Barnett's 1895 map of Athens shows several streets in the Baldwin/Baxter/Lumpkin area that no longer exist: Doboy, Narrow, Sapelo, and Summey.

Also shown in this view is the old water works on the west side of South Lumpkin Street, which was relocated next to the North Oconee River on the north side of town in the early 1890s (see Figure 10). In the mid-1920s construction was begun on Legion Pool, which opened at this site June 7, 1936.

Athens Streets & Neighborhoods

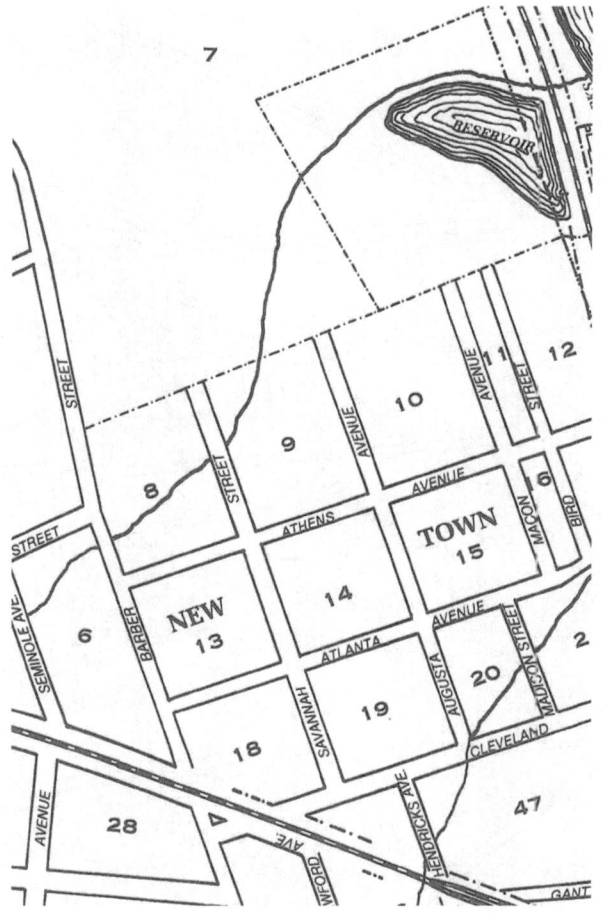

Figure 10. Barnett's 1895 map showing Newtown (seen here as New Town) was an African-American neighborhood developed on the North side of town in the early 1890s. An African-American school was opened in this neighborhood in 1911.

North of Newtown was Reese's Pond, which became the reservoir for the new Athens Water Works when that facility was moved from its old site on South Lumpkin Street (see Fig. 9).

Figure 11. Athens Park and Improvement Company shown on J. W. Barnett's 1895 map.

Athens Streets & Neighborhoods

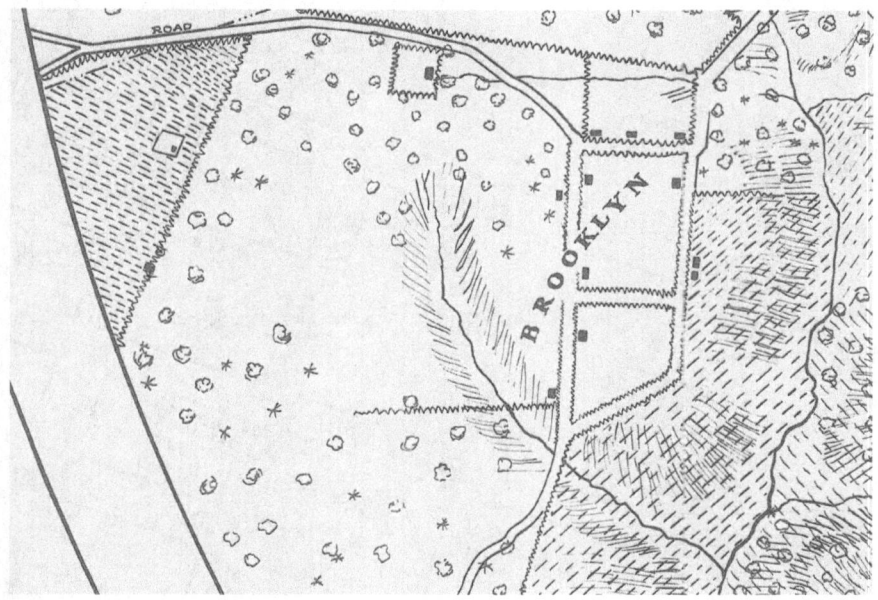

Figure 12. Thomas' 1874 map shows Brooklyn, a black neighborhood that prospered during the last quarter of the nineteenth century. When the community was established, Broad Street ended approximately where Alps Road and Hawthorne Avenue intersect it today. Brooklyn was located on the south side of this intersection, but in later times it was extended across present-day Broad Street along Hawthorne Avenue.

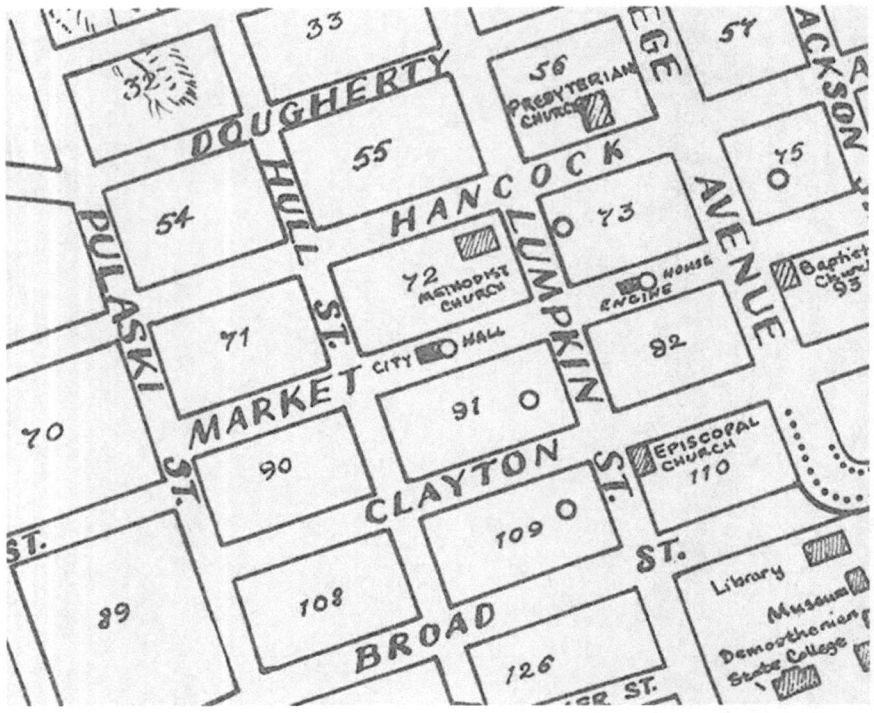

Figure 13. On W.W. Thomas' 1874 map, present day Washington Street is shown with its original name of Market Street. City Hall was in the middle of Market Street between Hull Street and Lumpkin Street. The Engine House was in the middle of Market Street between Lumpkin Street and College Avenue.

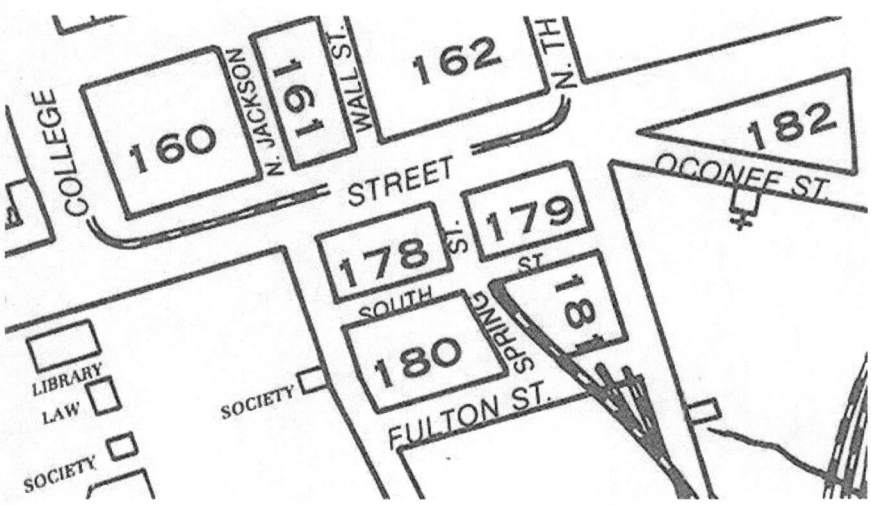

Figure 14. Granite Row or Granite Range is shown here on Barnett's 1895 map as block 178, It was located on the south side of East Broad Street between Spring Street on the East and South Jackson Street on the West.

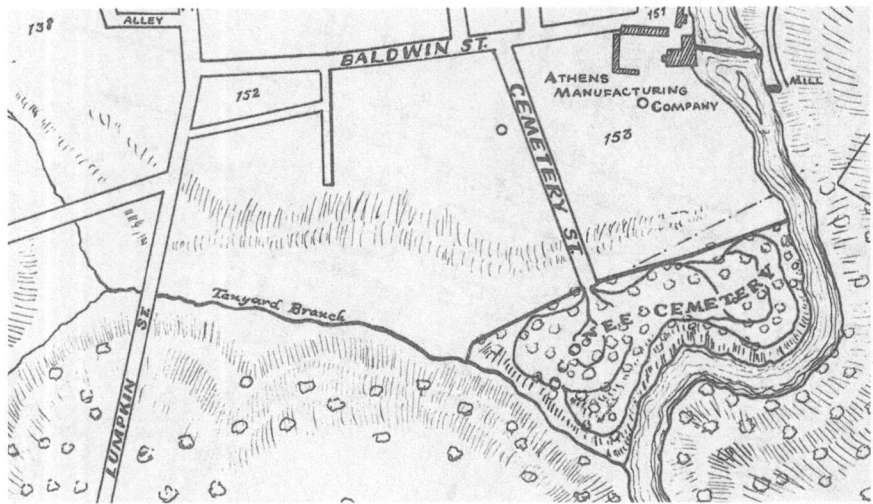

Figure 15. Thomas' 1874 map gives a good view of Tanyard Branch as it crossed Lumpkin Street and flows eastward to the border of Oconee Hill Cemetery and runs into the North Oconee River. Much of Tanyard Branch shown here now runs under Sanford Stadium.

Also shown here is Cemetery Street, which now bypasses Oconee Hill Cemetery and is named East Campus Drive.

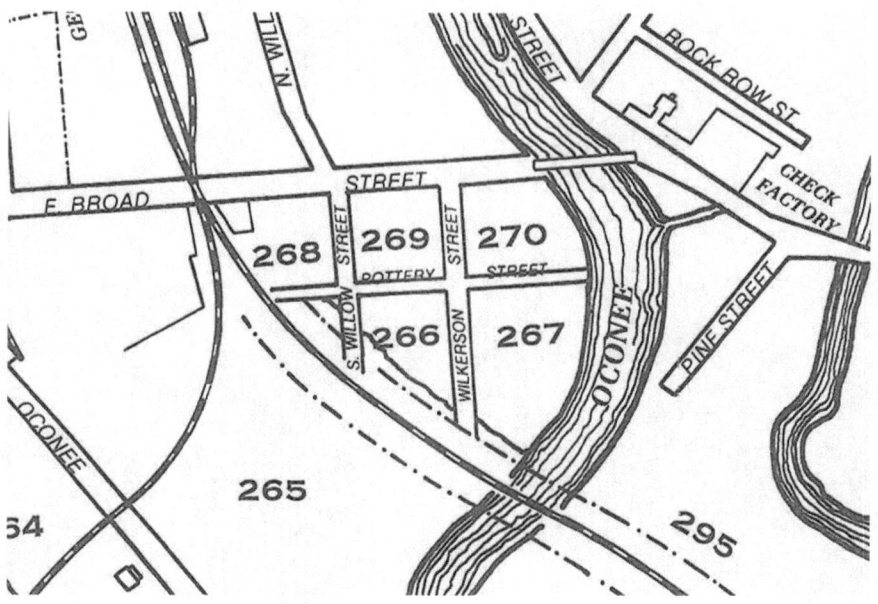

Figure 16. Barrett's 1895 map shows that Pottery Street originally ran east and west between the railroad and the North Oconee River and crossed Willow Street and Wilkerson Street.

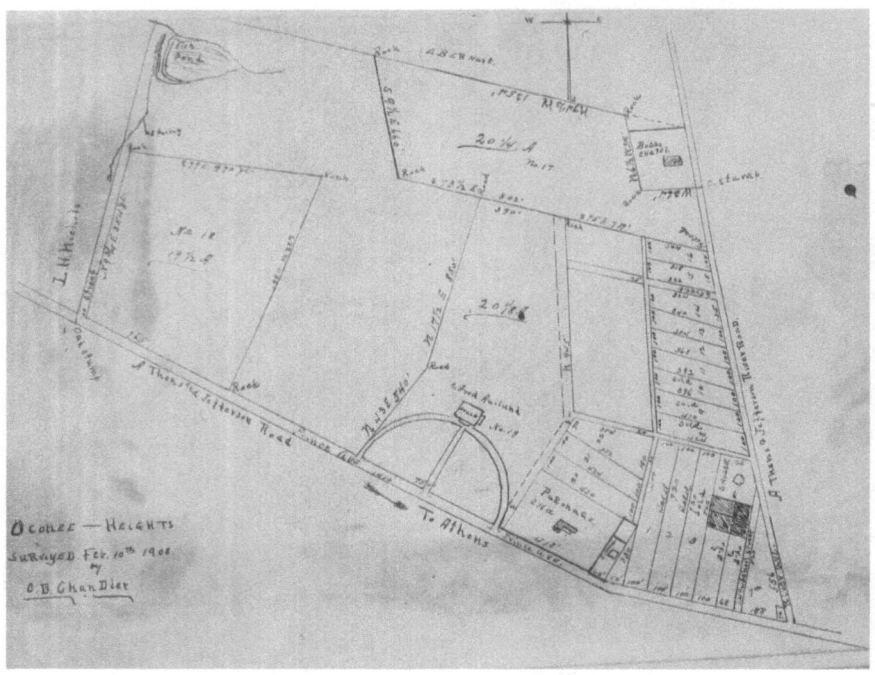

Figure 17. A plat of Oconee Heights made in 1908 shows the location of Fred and Anna Auslund's eleven-room mansion facing Prince Avenue (Athens & Jefferson Road), the school house facing Jefferson River Road, old Boggs Chapel, and much of the rest of the neighborhood. Clarke County Deed Book 1, page 577.

Athens Streets & Neighborhoods

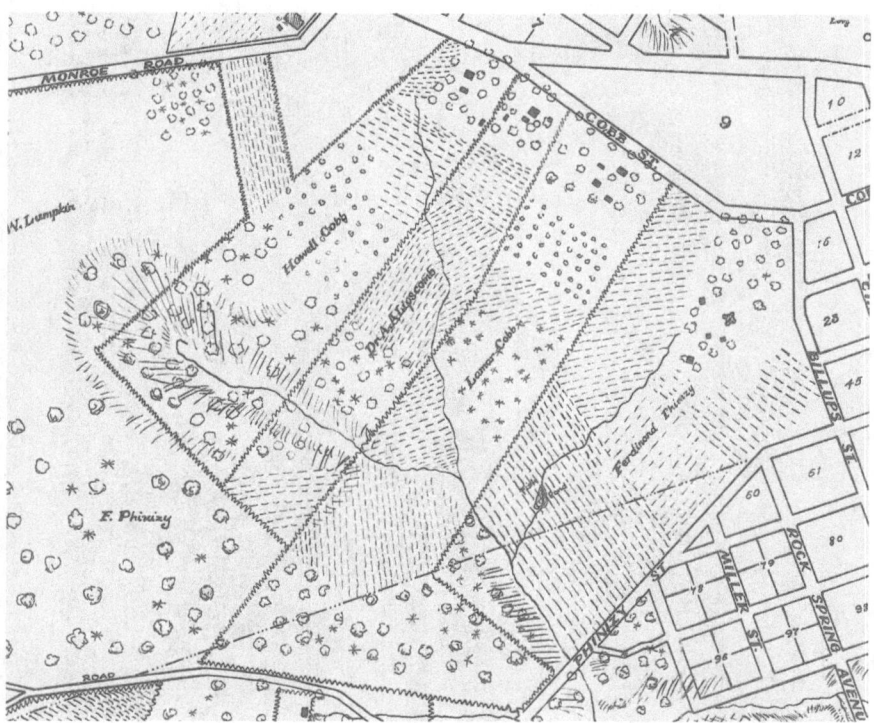

Figure 18. Thomas' 1874 map shows the general location of Camp Haskell, which fronted on Cobb Street and extended southwestward toward Broad Street. It was described as being between the J. S. King residence and the "old Phinizy place." That would locate it approximately where the properties of Dr. A. A. Lipscomb and Lamar Cobb are shown here.

Figure 19. Rare cabinet card photos of U.S. soldiers stationed at Camp Haskell in Athens during the Spanish-American War were made by Athens photographers.

This image is identified on the reverse as Sgt. George Thomas Fleming, Co. C., 15th Penn. Vol. Infantry.

Figure 20. An unidentified U.S. soldier holding a flute. Someone wrote on the back "Fifer, 3rd NJ, 2nd AC"

Because Sgt. Fleming, shown on the facing page, and this soldier were photographed by Athens photographers, there can be no doubt they were stationed at Camp Haskell in Athens during the Spanish-American War.

Gary L. Doster

Services at Camp Haskell,
ATHENS, GA, SUNDAY, JANUARY 22, 1899.

THIRD REG'T N. J. VOL. INF.

Conducted by CHAPLAIN J. MADISON HARE.

Voluntary by Band.

Doxology.

Lord's Prayer in Concert.

Hymn. ALL HAIL THE POWER OF JESUS' NAME.

All hail the pow'r of Jesus name,
Let angels prostrate fall;
Bring forth the royal diadem,
And crown Him Lord of all,

Let ev'ry kindred, ev'ry tribe,
On this terrestrial ball,
To Him all majesty ascribe,
And crown Him Lord of all.

Oh, that with yonder sacred throng,
We at His feet may fall;
We'll join the everlasting song,
And crown Him Lord of all.

23d PSALM IN CONCERT.

The Lord is my shepherd; I shall not want.
He maketh me to lie down in green pastures: he leadeth me beside the still waters.
He restoreth my soul; he leadeth me in paths of righteousness for his name's sake.
Yea, though I walk through the valley of the shadow of death, I will fear no evil; for thou art with me, thy rod and thy staff they comfort me.
Thou preparest a table before me in the presence of mine enemies: thou anointest my head with oil; my cup runneth over.
Surely goodness and mercy shall follow me all the days of my life: and I will dwell in the house of the Lord forever.

Prayer.

Hymn. JESUS LOVER OF MY SOUL.

Jesus, lover of my soul,
Let me to Thy bosom fly,
While the nearer water's roll,
While the tempest still is high!
Hide me, O, my Saviour hide,
Till the storm of life is past:
Safe into the haven guide,
Oh, receive my soul at last.

Thou, O Christ, art all I want;
More than all in thee I find,
Raise the fallen, cheer the faint,
Heal the sick! and lead the blind!
Just and holy is Thy Name,
I am all unrighteousness:
Vile and full of sin I am,
Thou art full of truth and grace

Sermon by CHAPLAIN HARE.

Hymn, AMERICA.

My country, 'tis of thee,
Sweet land of liberty,
Of thee I sing;
Land where my fathers died,
Land of the pilgrim's pride,
From ev'ry mountain side
Let freedom ring.

My native country, thee,
Land of the noble free;
Thy name I love,
I love thy rocks and rills,
Thy woods and templed hills
My heart with rapture thrills,
Like that above.

Let music swell the breeze;
And ring from all the trees
Sweet freedom's song;
Let mortal tongues awake,
Let all that breathe partake;
Let rocks their silence break.
The sound prolong.

Our father's God, to Thee,
Author of liberty,
To Thee we sing;
Long may our land be bright,
With freedom's holy light,
Protect us with thy might,
Great God, our King.

BENEDICTION.

Figure 21. A rare program for Sunday Services at Camp Haskell for January 22, 1899.

Figure 22. "The Heights"
W. S. Holman House
632 Oglethorpe Avenue

Index

This index is divided into three sections:

- People
- Streets and Roads
- Businesses, Communities, Neighborhoods, Organizations, and Places

People

Adams, Emma E. Barnett	1
Adams, Flora N. Williamson	3
Adams, Florida "Florrie" Virginia Wilkerson	3
Adams, Flournoy Woodbridge "Ferdy"	1
Adams, Habersham J.	1
Auslund, Anna Clark	100
Auslund, Christian Frederick	3, 98, 99, 100, 101
Bacon, Augustus Octavius	3
Bacon, Dr. William	3

Bailey, Thomas	3, 30
Bain, W. A.	30
Baker, Ernest	4
Baker, Grover	4
Baldwin, Abraham	4, 51
Barber, Greensby Wetherford "Wed"	5, 85
Barnett, Emma E.	1
Barnett, John	5
Barnett, John William	14
Barrett, Anne S.	60
Barrow, David Crenshaw, Jr.	5
Baxter, Thomas W.	6
Beacham, Jack	41
Becker, Carrie	6
Becker, John H.	6
Billups, Col. John	6
Billups, Sarah Jane	75
Blair, Martha J. Pridgeon	86
Blair, Merritt Ophelia	86
Blair, William D.	86
Bloomfield, Robert Lee	7, 62
Bondurant, John	92
Bone, Dorcas	87
Bone Family	87
Bowdre, Harriet Hays	60
Bowen, O. W.	102
Bray, Isham (or Isom) M.	10
Bray, Nora L.	10
Breedlove, Matilda Mozelle Jennings	43
Bridges, Jeff	30
Brightwell, Clara Talmage	55

Athens Streets & Neighborhoods

Brightwell, George Pierce	55
Brightwell, Nell Pierce	55
Brittain, Henry L.	10
Brooks, David William	11
Brown, Dr. John	12
Brown, Steven	83
Bryan, William Thomas	12
Burnett, Annie R. Jones	13
Burnett, Wiley Baxter	13
Cain, John R.	14
Carlton, Dr. Henry Hull	8, 14, 19, 36, 49, 50, 58
Carlton, Helen Camak Newton	36, 49, 58
Carlton, Marion	36
Carlton, Olivia	36
Carr, Cynthia Walker	91
Carr, Thomas	91
Carr, William Anthony	91
Caskey, Grandison Marion, Jr.	32, 49
Caskey, Grandison Marion, III	49
Caskey, Laura Ellen Jordan	32, 49
Chase, Albon	16
Childs, Asaph King	17, 33
Church, Alonzo	17
Clark, Anne	100
Clayton, Augustin Smith	18, 45, 56, 104
Clayton, Augusta Columbiana	45
Cleveland, President Stephen Grover	14
Clinton, George (U.S. vice-president)	21
Cobb, Howell, Sr.	20, 24, 66, 70
Cobb, John Addison	20, 91
Cobb, Lamar	88

Cobb, Laura Battaile	66
Cobb, Mary Ann Lamar	24
Cobb, Thomas Reade Rootes	43
Cohen, Aaron	20
Cohen, Julius	20
Coleman, Dr. Kenneth	93
Conway, Dr. William Buchanan	30
Cook Brothers	79
Cook, Ferdinand	2
Cook, Francis	2
Crawford, Hiram Hayes	21
Crawford, William Harris	21
Crews, M. B.	102
Crews, W. W.	102
Daniell, Henrietta Virginia Jennings	42
Davenport, Nancy Jennings	43
Dearing, William	22, 104
Dobbs, Burney Springer	22
Dobbs, Stephen C.	22
Dorsey, Mayor	44
Doster, Walter Lafayette	95
Dougherty, Judge Charles	23
Dozier, Thomas Howard, Sr.	30
Driftmier, Rudolph Henry	91
DuBose, Robert Toombs	23
Dudley, Alonzo Gordon "Lon"	24
Easley, Daniel W.	91
Epps, Benjamin Thomas, Sr.	24
Epps, Cecilia Penelope Jennings	43
Epps, Sarah Alexander	24
Epps, William	24

Athens Streets & Neighborhoods

Espy, James (also seen as Espey)	25
Espy, John (also seen as Espey)	25
Finley, Dr. Robert	26
Flanigen, Cameron Douglas	62
Forbes, Walter T.	70
Forbes, Willie Marion Stanton	70
Forsyth, John	7
Fortson, Judge Blanton Erwin, Sr.	27
Fowler Family	93
Franklin, Leonidas	27
Franklin, Marcus A.	77
Fulton, James	28
Gantt, Thomas Lawrence "Larry"	18, 19, 28, 98
Garwood, Jonathan	30
Gean Family	87
Gilleland, John Wesley, Sr.	29, 30
Gilmer, Governor George Rockingham	31
Godfrey, Robert Wiley (also seen as Godfree and Godfrie)	9
Grady, Henry Woodfin	31, 45
Grady, Julia King	45
Grady, William Sammons	31
Graves, B. M.	103
Green, Dr. William	33
Hampton, Col. T. C.	18
Hancock, Thomas	34
Harris, Jeptha Vining	35
Harris, Joel Chandler	70
Harris, Stephen Willis	35
Harris, Young Loftin Gerdine	35
Harsha, T. R.	62
Harsha, W. A.	62

Hart, Nancy	36
Haskell, Brig. Gen. Joseph Theodore	88
Hayes, President Rutherford Birchard	18
Haygood, Oscar Williford	102
Henderson, Dr. Matthew Henry	36
Hendricks, Thomas Andrews	18, 37
Hendrix, E. E.	103
Herring, John Newton	37
Herty, Dr. Charles Holmes	37
Hester, Al	95
Hill, Ann Scott	72
Hill, Sen. Benjamin Harvey	38
Hill, Blanton Meade	38
Hinton, F. B.	62
Hodgson, Asbury Hull	39
Hodgson Family	39
Holman, William Shrewsbury	40, 89, 98
Hoyt, Dr. Nathan	40
Hull, Asbury	41, 43
Hull, Augustus Longstreet	8, 19, 80
Ingle, J. W.	65, 102
Jackson, Dr. Henry	42
Jacobson, Rosa C. Stern	97
Jennings Family	42, 43
Jones, Annie R.	13
Jordan, J. T.	102
Key, Sarah	61, 72
King, Augusta Columbiana Clayton	45
King, James Sebastian	44, 99
King, Sarah C.	99
King, Dr. William C.	44

Athens Streets & Neighborhoods

Langford, Cynthia Ann Jennings	43
Leathers, Milton	78, 92
LeConte, James	45
LeConte, John	45
Lilly Family	87
Lilly, Edward	87
Little, Mr.	30
Long, Dr. Crawford Williamson	46
Long, Dr. Henry Russell Jones	46
Low, William	91
Lucas, F. W.	83
Lumpkin, Edwin King	13
Lumpkin, Joseph Henry	17, 57
Lumpkin, Wilson	46
Lyndon, Dr. Edward Smith	45, 47
Mabry Family	87
Madison, President James	21
Mann, Horace	98
Marshall, Charlotte	52
Martin, Susan Brittain	11
Matthews, Frances America Jennings	43
McWhorter, Judge Hamilton	19, 50
Meeker, John Armstrong	19
Mell, Edward Baker	51
Mell Family	72
Mell, John Dagg	51
Mell, Patrick Hues	51
Meigs, Josiah	50
Milledge, John	51
Mitchell, Thomas	52
Mitchell, William Letcher (hotel keeper & postmaster)	52

Mitchell, William Letcher "Slickhead" (lawyer)	52
Mizelle, Patrick	30
Morris, Casper	53
Morris, Sylvanus	19
Morton, John White	54
Morton, Monroe Bowers "Pink"	95
Morton, Rosena White	54
Morton, William J.	54
Newton, Catherine Lowrance	80
Newton, Elizur Lowrance	55
Newton, Helen Carmak	36, 49, 58
Newton, John Hamlin	8, 36, 49, 55, 58
Newton, Mary Jordan	36, 49, 58
Nichols, Louis Harrison	66, 101
Nicholson, John William	31, 56
Nisbet, Eugenius Aristides	56
Nisbet, John	104
O'Farrell, Ed	57
O'Farrell, James	57
O'Farrell, William Daniel	57
Parr, General Daniel	86
Parr, Merritt Ophelia Blair	86
Peabody, George Foster	59
Peters, Richard	59
Phinizy, Barrett	5
Phinizy Family	10, 42, 46, 60, 71
Phinizy, Ferdinand	5, 60, 88
Pope, Maj. Gen. Burwell, Jr.	7, 61
Pope, Charles	61
Pope, Sarah Key Strong	61
Pound, Jere Madison	62

Athens Streets & Neighborhoods

Pridgeon, Martha J.	86
Prince, Garland W.	101, 102
Prince, John	101
Prince, Noah	101
Prince, Noah F.	101
Prince Family	101
Prince, Oliver Hillhouse	63
Pulaski, Count Casimir	64
Quillian, Rev. H. M.	74
Ramsaur, Claude	103
Randall, Brig. Gen. George Morton	89
Reap, James K.	85
Reaves, Edward Augustus	56
Reed, Thomas Walter	7
Reese, Dr. Charles Milton	64
Reynolds, Susan Mayne Jennings	43
Rhodes, Alexander Stephens	65, 100
Rowland, Charles A. IV	94
Russell, Lewis C.	76
Russell, Richard Bevard, Jr.	66, 76
Russell, Richard Bevard, Sr.	66, 76
Russell, Judge William John	66, 76
Rutherford, Laura Battaile Cobb	66
Rutherford, Williams	66
Rutherford, Williams, Jr.	11
Sanford, Dr. Steadman Vincent	66
Saye, A. H.	4
Sikes, Prudence Elizabeth Jennings	42
Smith, Edward Inglis, Sr.	68
Smith, Paul Lloyd	68
Soule, Andrew McNairn	69

Spalding, Dr. Phinizy	92
Stanton, Lucy May	65, 69, 70
Stanton, Willie Marion	70
Stegeman, Herman James	70
Stephens, Alexander Hamilton	71
Stern, Rosa C.	97
Strong, Ann Scott Hill	72
Strong, Charles	72
Strong, Elisha	72
Strong, Sarah Key	61, 72
Summey, Peter A.	73
Talmadge, Clovis Gerdine	74
Talmadge, John	74
Talmadge, John Emmeus, Sr.	30
Taylor, Gen. Robert	13, 75
Taylor, Richard Deloney Bolling	31, 75
Taylor, Sarah Jane Billups	75
Thomas, Stevens	75
Thomas, William Winstead	104
Tibbetts, John Francis	75
Tilden, Samuel Jones	18, 76
Treanor, Katharine McKinley Taylor	11
Tweety, Mr.	30
Upson, Judge Stephen Cummins	77
Waddel, James Pleasants	77
Waddel, Moses	77
Waddel, William Henry	77
Walker, Abram	104
Walker, Cynthia	91
Ware, Dr. Edward Roswell	47, 78
Warner, Hiram	56
Washington, President George	78
Weeks, Eve B.	84, 96
Westmoreland Family	87
White, John	79, 80, 85, 103

Athens Streets & Neighborhoods

White, John Richards	104
Wilkerson, Florida "Florrie" Virginia	33
Wilkerson, Col. Isaac	80
Wilkins, John J.	91
Williams, George	62
Williams, William	81
Williamson, Flora N.	33
Winter, John	105
Woods, Elizabeth Groves	81
Woods, Emma Ellice	81
Woods, Emma Conger	81
Woods, Mary Etta	81
Woods, Joseph White	81
Wray, Thomas	82
Wynne, Young H.	56

Streets and Roads:

Adams Street	1, 3, 33, 81
Agriculture Drive	11
Airport Road	60
Alley No. 2	75
Alps Road	87
Ambler Road	2, 3, 65, 101
Annes Court	84
Armory Road	2, 79
Athens Avenue	97
Atlanta Avenue	7, 71, 97
Augusta Alley	2, 6
Augusta Avenue	2, 6, 27, 97
Auslund Avenue	2, 3, 100, 101
Bacon Street	3
Bailey Street	3
Bailey Row	3

Baker Street	4
Baldwin Street	4, 23, 37, 42, 55, 56, 66, 79, 81
Barber Street	5, 9, 15, 16, 21, 30, 38, 46, 54, 58, 67, 68, 71, 82, 84, 85, 97
Barnett Shoals Road	5, 8
Barrett Street	5, 40, 46, 65, 66, 71, 81
Barrow Street	5
Baxter Drive	6, 24
Baxter Street	6, 17, 35, 40, 61
Becker Street	6, 26
Bernside Alley	2, 6
Berry Street	6, 10, 39
Billups Street	6, 78, 88
Bird Street	7, 97
Bloomfield Street	7
Bobbin Mill Road	8, 27, 50
Bob Godfrey Road	5, 8, 9, 102
Belmont Road	9
Boulevard, The	9, 14, 20, 47, 59, 75, 82, 85, 97
Bowdre Street	9, 10, 19, 31, 42, 46, 50, 51, 60, 71
Branch Street	34, 68, 73
Bray's Alley	10
Bremond (or Bremont) Street	10
Bridge Street	6, 10, 39
Brittain Avenue	10
Broad Street	11, 17, 20, 21, 22, 25, 26, 28, 35, 36, 37, 39, 40, 42, 43, 44, 46, 50, 52, 53, 57, 60, 61, 64, 68, 69, 73, 75, 77, 78, 80, 87, 88, 94
Brookwood Drive	38
Brown Street	12, 32, 48
Bryan Street	12, 13, 51
Bryant Street	13
Buena Vista Avenue	13, 24, 82
Burnett Avenue	13
Cain Street	14, 97

Athens Streets & Neighborhoods

Carlton Avenue, Street, Road, Terrace	14, 36, 49, 57
Carr Street	15
Castalia Avenue	15
Catawba Avenue	15
Cedar Drive	11
Cedar Street	46, 66
Cemetery Street	15, 56
Chase Street	12, 15, 16, 17, 46, 51, 58, 63, 95, 97
Chattooga Avenue (also Chatooga Avenue)	16, 74
Chatuga Avenue	17, 74, 81
Cherokee Avenue	15
Cherry Street	17, 23, 97
Childs Street	17
Church Street	17, 34, 47, 68, 101
Clarkesville Road	17, 20
Clayton Street	18, 40, 77
Cleveland Avenue	18, 19, 21, 28, 37, 64, 69, 76
Clover Street	9, 19, 38, 39, 40, 42, 46, 50, 71
Cloverhurst Avenue	17, 19, 34, 50, 91
Cobb Street	16, 20, 38, 44, 63, 87, 88
Cohen Street	20, 97
College Avenue	3, 20, 31, 47, 72, 78, 81
Commerce Road	18, 20, 39
Compress Street	20
Crawford Avenue	21
Danielsville Road	37, 47
Dearing Street	15, 22, 27
Derby Street	37
Devil's Ford Road	22
Dobbs Street	22
Doboy Street	23, 55, 66
Dr. Martin Luther King, Jr. Parkway	2, 23, 39, 50, 72, 79
Dougherty Street	23, 40, 78
Dublin Street	73
DuBose Avenue	17, 23, 47, 97

Dudley Drive	24
D. W. Brooks Drive	11, 34, 47, 69
East Campus Drive	15, 24, 57
East Campus Road	11, 56
Epps Bridge Road	24, 45
Espy Street (also seen as Espey)	25
Elizabeth Street	5, 24, 66
Erwin Street	24
Factory Street	25, 53
Fairview Avenue	53
Fairview Street	4, 78
Federal Road	13, 25, 63, 92
Ferdinand Street	26, 60
Finley Street (also spelled Findley and Findly)	22, 26
Flint Street	26
Florida Avenue	6, 26
Forbstein Alley (also seen as Farbstein, Farbtein, and Forestein)	26
Fortson Drive	24, 27, 88
Foundry Street	27, 80
Fourth Street	26
Fowler Avenue	27
Front Street	11, 20, 28, 94
Franklin Street	27
Fuller Street	27, 28
Fulton Street	28
Gantt Street	18, 19, 28, 75
Georgia Depot Street	28, 76
Georgia Drive	15, 28, 76
Georgia Factory Road	14, 29, 83, 85
Gilleland Drive	29
Gilmer Street	31, 80
Glenhaven Avenue	10, 31, 50
Grace Street	31
Grady Avenue	17, 23, 31
Gran Ellen Drive	32, 49, 60, 83

Athens Streets & Neighborhoods

Graveyard Street	12, 32, 48
Green Street	32, 34
Griffith Street	33
Habersham Street	1, 33, 57
Hall Street	34
Hampton Avenue	34, 53, 68
Hampton Court	34, 68, 83
Hancock Avenue	32, 34, 38, 40, 42, 46, 60, 71, 88, 97
Harper Street	34
Harris Street	35
Hart Avenue	36
Hawthorne Avenue	31, 87
Helen Street	36, 49, 57
Henderson Avenue	36, 70
Hendricks Avenue	18, 28, 37, 64, 75
Herring Street	34, 37, 50
Herty Drive	37
Hiawassee Avenue	38, 75
Highland Avenue	15
Hill Street	17, 38, 65
Hillcrest Avenue	9, 19, 38, 39, 42, 46, 50, 71, 97
Hobson Avenue	39, 79
Hodgson Drive	36, 39
Hodgson Street	6, 10, 39
Holman Avenue	40, 43
Hoyt Street	40
Hughes Avenue	40, 65
Hull Street	26, 30, 40, 72, 80, 81
Ingle Street	41
Inglewood Avenue	41, 102, 103
Jackson Street	12, 15, 25, 28, 32, 37, 41, 47, 48, 51, 61, 72, 77, 94, 95, 101
Jacob Street	40, 42, 60
Jefferson River Road	99
Jefferson Road	98

Jennings Mill Road	42
John Street	43
Johns Street	43
Jonas Avenue	43
King Avenue	20, 36, 38, 39, 40, 43, 44, 45
LeConte Avenue	45
Lenoir Avenue	45
Leonard Street	46, 60
Long Avenue	46, 71
Lumpkin Street	10, 27, 31, 32, 34, 40, 46, 52, 55, 64, 67, 68, 70, 73, 78, 80, 85, 86, 92, 101
Lyndon Avenue	14, 20, 23, 47, 53, 97
Lyndon Row	47
Macon Avenue	2, 6, 27, 97
Macon Highway	101
Madison Avenue	5, 10, 41, 46, 47, 57, 65, 66, 71, 72, 79, 81
Magazine Street	12, 32, 48, 49
Marion Drive	32, 49
Marion Street	36, 49, 57
Market Street	50, 79
Marlin Street	50
Matthews Avenue	10, 50
McWhorter Street	5
Mealor Street	50
Meigs Street	9, 50, 92
Mell Street	51
Miles Street	51
Milledge Avenue	1, 19, 25, 26, 29, 32, 33, 34, 35, 36, 49, 51, 52, 56, 58, 60, 72, 80, 83, 84, 85, 86 92, 96
Milledge Avenue Extension	60, 83
Milledge Circle	15, 52, 85, 92
Milledge Terrace	83
Miller Street	52
Mitchell Bridge Road	52, 89
Mitchell Street—previous	25, 52

Athens Streets & Neighborhoods

Mitchell Street—present	49, 53
Morris Street	47, 53, 97
Morton Avenue	26, 53, 68, 96
Morton Street	53
Nacoochee Avenue	16, 54, 75, 77
Nantahala Avenue	54, 62
Narrow Street	55
Nellie B Avenue	55
Newton Street	47, 55
Nichols Street	55, 100, 101
Nicholson Street	56
Nisbet Street	15, 24, 56
North Avenue	5, 10, 46, 47, 50, 57, 65, 66, 71, 72, 79, 81, 85
Oak Street	15, 29, 41, 73
Oakland Avenue	2, 15, 33, 57
Oaktree Street	31
Oconee Street	3, 7, 15, 29, 44, 53, 57, 59, 76, 80, 81
Odd Street	26, 33, 43
O'Farrell Street	57
Oglethorpe Avenue	29, 40, 89, 93, 98
Olivia Street	36, 49, 57
Onedia Street or Oneida Street	58
Park Avenue	58
Peabody Street	35, 59
Peter Street	4, 37, 59
Peters Street	59
Phinizy Street	5, 26, 40, 42, 46, 59, 66, 71, 88
Phoenix Road	22
Pinecrest Court	60, 83
Pinecrest Drive	96
Plantation Road	60, 83
Plum Nelly Road	60
Pope Street	61
Pottery Street	61

Pound Street	9, 62
Prince Avenue	3, 13, 14, 16, 17, 20, 23, 24, 25, 27, 31, 35, 38, 45, 47, 51, 52, 54, 58, 61, 62, 63, 67, 68, 75, 77, 79, 82, 84, 92, 93, 97, 98
Prince Avenue Extension	93
Prince Place	16, 63
Princeton Factory Road	46, 64, 85
Princeton Road	46, 64, 85
Public Street	11, 64
Pulaski Heights	64, 102
Pulaski Street	18, 28, 38, 64, 67, 75
Reese Street	27, 64, 67, 75
Rhodes Street	2, 65, 101
River Street	5, 10, 46, 47, 57, 65, 66
Rocksprings Street	22, 52, 60, 65, 67, 78, 81
Roseland Street	65, 69
Russell Avenue	40, 65
Ruth Street	5, 24, 40, 43, 46, 65, 66, 71, 79, 81
Rutherford Street	1, 27, 33, 36, 49, 51, 58, 66, 72, 80
Sanford Drive	23, 66, 69
Sapelo Street	23, 55, 66, 73
Satula Avenue (first spelled Satulah)	67
Satulah Avenue (now spelled Satula)	67
Savannah Street	97
School Street	55, 65, 67, 75, 101
Scott Street	68
Seminole Avenue	68
Simons Street	68
Simonton Bridge Road	51, 86
Smith Street	27, 68
Soule Street	11, 68

South Georgia Avenue	105
South View Drive	56, 68
Spring Street	69, 94
Springdale Street	8, 51
Standard Oil Road	69
Standard Oil Street	69
Stanton Way	65, 69
States' Rights Street	36, 70
Stegeman Drive	70
Stephens Street	71
Stevens Street	71
Stewart Street	39, 60, 71
Strickland Street	10, 39, 50, 72
Stonewall Avenue	46, 71
Strong Street	6, 39, 72
Summey Street	73
Tabernacle Street	73
Tallulah Avenue	17, 74
Tallulah Street	74, 79
Talmadge Drive	74
Talmadge Street	74
Taylor Street	65, 67, 75
The Plaza	39, 65
Third Street	26, 33, 43
Thomas Street	12, 18, 32, 47, 48, 53, 57, 65, 75, 77, 81
Tibbets Avenue	28
Tibbetts Street	28
Tilden Street	18, 76
Timothy Road	66, 76
Trilby Street	76
University Drive	96

Upson's Alley

	76
Vine Street	4, 78
Waddell Street	26, 28, 77
Wall Street	77
Walton Street	23, 78
Wanassed Street	78
Ware Street	78
Warren Street	78
Washington Street	50, 78
Water Street	2, 5, 23, 39, 47, 57, 65, 66, 79
Watkinsville Road	46, 64, 79, 85
West Lake Drive	27, 60, 87
West View Drive	17, 74, 79
Westview Drive	50, 60
White Avenue	79, 80
White Street	30, 53, 80
Whitehall Road	51, 83
Wilcox Street	80
Wilkerson Street	61, 80
Williams Street	25, 53, 79, 81
Willow Street	20, 61, 72
Winterville Road	55, 59
Wolfskin Road	9
Woodland Way	17, 74, 81
Woodlawn Avenue	2, 50, 81
Woods Avenue	46, 71, 81
Wray Street	81
Wynbourne Avenue	82
Wynburn Avenue	82
Wynburn Place	82
Yonah Avenue	13, 24, 82

Businesses, Communities, Neighborhoods, Organizations, and Places

Adams Estate	1, 33
African-American church	84, 87
African-American school	84, 87
African-American neighborhood	83, 97
African Baptist Church	25
Allenville — also seen as Alenville	83, 84
AMVETS Post	10 55
Armstrong & Dobbs	22
Arnoldsville, GA	72
Athens Carriage and Wagon Works	79
Athens Chamber of Commerce	44
Athens City Council	43, 44, 49
Athens City Directory	4, 6, 13, 14, 21, 22, 35, 50, 54, 58, 71, 73, 74, 86
Athens-Clarke County Fire Station No. 1	96
Athens Country Club	24
Athens Electric Railway Company	13
Athens Factory	7, 25
Athens Foundry and Machine Works	3, 27
Athens High and Industrial School	94
Athens High School	51
Athens Historical Society	84, 96, 98
Athens Latino Mission United Methodist Church	99
Athens Manufacturing Company	6, 25, 37
Athens Park and Improvement Company	9, 16, 38, 46, 54, 58, 67, 68, 75, 82, 84
Athens Post Office	52
Athens Pottery	61
Athens Railway & Electric Company	75
Athens Steam Company	3, 27, 73
Athens Street Railway Company	84, 89
Athens Women's Suffrage League	70

Athens Y.W.C.A.	70
Bank of America	40
Bank of Athens	73
Barber Creek	92
Barberville Community	5, 85
Barnesville, GA	62, 63
Barnett Shoals Dam	5, 9
Barrow Elementary School	5
Barrow Hall	5
Bernardos	25
Blairsville Community	85
Boggs Chapel Methodist Church	99
Brooklyn Branch	8, 87, 88
Brooklyn Cemetery	87
Brooklyn Community	87, 88
Buena Vista Farm	13
Buenavista, Mexico	13
Camak Manufacturing Company	101, 102
Camp Haskell	87, 88, 89, 90
Camp Wilkins	90, 91, 104
Carr's Hill	15, 59, 91
Catawba Indians	15
Charity of Love Cemetery	84
Chase Street School	46
Chatuga River	16
Chattooga River	16
Cherokee Indians	46
Chicopee Mill	79
Childs & Nickerson Hardware	17
Church's "Homeplace"	83
Clarke Central High School	78
Clarke Cotton Mills	103
Clayton County, GA	18
Cloverhurst Farm	19, 91
Cobb County, GA	35

Athens Streets & Neighborhoods

Cobbham	20, 70, 91, 92, 97
College Avenue School	72
Commerce, GA	17
Confederate Army	6, 53
Confederate Cross of Honor	24
Cook and Brother Armory	2, 79
Cord Mill	92
Cord Mill Community	92
Cotton States Mutual Insurance Company	12
Cox College	69
Crawford, GA	22
Crawfordville, GA	71
Daughters of the American Revolution	29
Digital Library of Georgia, The	107
Dillard, GA	104
Distinguished Agribusiness Award	12
Doboy Sound	23, 67
Double-barreled cannon	3, 29, 30
Dougherty County, GA	23
Driftmier Agriculture Engineering Center	91
D. W. Brooks Lecture Series	12
D. W. Brooks Mall	11
Earth Fare	86
East Athens	3, 4, 15, 26, 33, 35, 37, 41, 43, 50, 59, 68, 78, 91, 102
East Athens Methodist Church	73
Emmanuel Episcopal Church	7
Epps Bridge Road	24, 44
Factory Burying Ground	37
Farmers Hardware	44
Filehne, Germany	53
First Baptist Church	22, 38
First Methodist Church	34
First National Bank of Athens	54
First Presbyterian Church	25

Five Points	1, 15, 33, 52, 83, 85, 86, 92, 93, 96
Fowler's Junction	93
Fowler Town or Fowler's Town	93
Franklin College	4, 20
Franklin House (hotel)	52
Georgia Factory	14, 29, 80, 83, 85, 103
Georgia Rail Road	29, 81
Georgia Rail Road and Banking Company	22
Georgia Railroad Depot	80
Georgia Secession Convention	43
Georgia Senate	7, 23
Georgia State College for Women	62
Georgia State Schools	62
Georgia State Women's College at Valdosta, GA	62
Gold Kist, Inc.	12
Good Templars Lodge	86
Gouvain-Newton house	81
Granite Range	94
Granite Row	28, 94
Happy Top	95
Harmony Grove	17
Hiawassee	38, 46, 67
Hodgson Brothers	74
Holy Cross Evangelical Lutheran Church	87
Holman Hotel	40
Hot Corner	95
Hotel Indigo	72, 96
Hull-Snelling House	41
Inferior Court of Clarke County	43
Irish revolution of 1799	33
J. S. King and Company	44
Jackson County	98
Jackson Street Cemetery	95, 101
Jefferson County, GA	20, 34
Joseph Henry Lumpkin House	17

Athens Streets & Neighborhoods

Lake Herrick	84
Lampkin & Adams	33
Lampkin/Charbonnier/Ashe House	51
LeConte Hall	45
Liberty Hill, GA	62
Lickskillet	96
Lilly Park	96
Lintons Spring	5
Lipscomb Volunteers	1
Lumpkin & Burnett law firm	14
Lyndon House Arts Center	47
Lynwood Park	97, 100
Madison, GA	35, 92
Main Street Bank	75
Mallison Braided Cord Company	92
McGregor Company	41
McNutt Creek	42, 92
Mecklenburg County, NC	103
Medical College of Georgia	98
Meigs Hall	5
Memorial Park	32
Metropolitan Museum of Art	70
Mexican War	13
Milledgeville, GA	43, 51, 62
Mitchell Bridge Road	52, 89
Mitchell Thunderbolts	7, 29, 73
Mitchell's Mills	52
Monroe County, MS	72
Morristown	14, 17, 20, 47, 53, 97
Morton Theater	95
Museum of Fine Arts	70
National Bank of Athens	1, 17, 80
National Portrait Gallery	70
New Jersey	7, 26, 101
New Jersey Regiment, Third	89, 90

New Orleans	2, 44
New Town or Newtown	2, 6, 7, 27
Newnan, GA	47
New York	1, 58, 59, 70, 77, 88
New York Volunteers, Second	89
Nicholson, Reaves & Wynne	56
Normal Heights	98
Normal School or State Normal School	62, 63, 93, 98
Normaltown	98
Oconee Heights	2, 3, 17, 55, 56, 65, 67, 68, 98, 100, 101
Oconee Hill Cemetery	2, 15, 37, 52, 55, 61, 70, 72, 96
Oconee River, Middle	65, 101, 102, 103
Oconee River, North	3, 5, 6, 10, 22, 31, 39, 47, 57, 61, 66, 78, 79, 80, 85, 91, 96, 97, 103
Old Athens Cemetery	12, 25, 32, 48, 61, 95, 101
Old Madison Cemetery	35
Oneida Indians	58
Phinizy Branch	88
Phinizy place	88, 125
Pineland Cemetery in Sebring, FL	100
Pioneer Paper Mill	92
Prince's Bridge	102
Pound Auditorium	62
Princeton College	6
Princeton Factory	46, 54, 64, 81, 85, 101, 102
Prince Town	102
Progressive Farmer's Man of the Year in Agriculture in the South	12
Pulaski Heights	64, 102
Puritan Cordage Mills — Mallison Division	92
Revolutionary War	5, 25, 36, 72, 102
Richard Deloney Bolling Taylor House	31
Royston, GA	11
St. Mary's Episcopal Church	7
St. Mary's Hospital	35
Sandy Creek Church	25

Athens Streets & Neighborhoods

Sanford Stadium	66, 70
Santiago, Battle of	89
Sapelo Island, GA	23, 67
Sapelo Sound	23, 67
Satulah Mountain	NC 67
Science Hall	45
Seaboard Airline Railroad	48, 93
Seminole Indian War	6, 7
Six-Mile Station	102, 105
Sledge-Cobb-Spalding House	44
Smithsonian Institution	70
South Carolina	13, 15, 21, 45, 88, 103
Southern Cotton Association	44
Southern Female College	69
Southern Manufacturing Company	13, 95
Southern Mill	75
Southern Mutual Insurance Company	13, 16, 35, 41
Spanish-American War	87, 88, 89
Star Thread Factory	5, 54
State Normal School	62, 63, 93, 98
State Normal School and Teachers College	62
Stegeman Coliseum	71
Stegeman Hall	70, 71
Summey & Newton	73
Sundsvall, Sweden	99
Tallulah Falls	16, 74
Talmadge Brothers	74
Talmadge, Hodgson & Company	74
Tanyard Branch	23, 85
Tate Student Center	23, 66
Taylor-Grady House	31, 75
Thankful Baptist Church	84
Timothy grass	76
Timothy hay	76
Timothy Heights	66, 76

Town Hall and Market House	78
Treanor House	10, 11
Trust Company Bank of Northeast Georgia	77
Union College	6
Union Point	12, 16, 56
United Daughters of the Confederacy	24
University Demonstration School	63
VonCannon-Wall Building	34
War Between the States 1. 2.	6, 7, 32, 40. 53, 59, 72, 73, 79, 89
War of 1812	33, 35, 61, 73
Ware-Lyndon House	47, 96
Watkinsville, GA	79, 86
Webb-Crawford Company	21
West Virginia Land Company	97
White City	41, 102
White City Manufacturing Company	41, 102
White Hall	104
Whitehall	14, 22, 29, 51, 80, 83, 85, 86, 103
Wilkerson Place	80
Winters	104, 105
Winter's Station	104, 105
Winter Ville	104, 105
Winterville	102, 104, 105
Wray-Nicholson House	82
Young Harris, GA	35

About the Author

Gary Doster is a native Athenian and has been interested in history since he was a small child. He collects Georgia historical artifacts, which includes a large collection of material concerning Athens. Doster has authored eight other books using material from his collections, and he co-authored another book with one of his granddaughters. He also has contributed material to several other books, including writing the Foreword to two of them. Doster worked for the Southeastern Cooperative Wildlife Disease Study, headquartered at the University of Georgia's College of Veterinary Medicine, for 46 years. At this job, he authored or co-authored 40 scientific articles in journals and textbooks and retired as a Research Coordinator. Doster has been married to the former Faye Ann Thomas of Oconee County for 61 years. They have three sons, three grandsons, three granddaughters, and, to date, have three great-granddaughters.

www.ingramcontent.com/pod-product-compliance
Lightning Source LLC
Chambersburg PA
CBHW030332230426
43661CB00032B/1386/J